Ifs, Ands, & Buts
CHILDREN'S SERMONS

BY Mary Grace Becker
and
Susan Martins Miller

NexGen® is an imprint of
Cook Communications Ministries, Colorado Springs, CO 80918
Cook Communications, Paris, Ontario

IFS, ANDS, AND BUTS CHILREN'S SERMONS
© 2005 by Cook Communications Ministries

First printing 2005
Printed in the Untied States of America
1 2 3 4 5 6 7 8 9 10 Printing/Year 00 09 08 07 05

Product Development Manager: Karen Pickering
Illustrations by Aline L. Heiser, Heiser Graphics
Photography © SW Productions
Cover design by Peter Schmidt and Scot McDonald, Granite Design
Interior design by Dana Sherrer, idesignetc
Interior production by Granite Design

ISBN: 0781442060

Table of Contents

IFs

ANDs

BUTs

You Have What You Need

Look at what you can do with stuff you've already got around the house! The children's sermons in this book use ordinary, easy-to-find supplies as a jumping-off point for life-changing lessons in God's Word. Here's everything you need for all the sermons in this book.

Aluminum foil
Apron with pockets
Baby pictures
Baking soda
Ball (red, small)
Beach ball
Beanbags
Blankets
Bubble wrap or packing peanuts
Cardboard square, 3' x 3'
Cell phone
Chalk
Checkerboard
Cleaning supplies
Cotton balls
Craft sticks
Dessert bowls
Dryer sheets (used)
Extracts (vanilla, mint, lemon)
Glass jar
Glue

Highlighter
Index cards, plain and colored
Jackets
Large box
Laundry bag
Lemon
Markers
Masking tape
Matches
Mirrors
Nonperishable foods
Paper clips
Paper grocery sack
Paper plates (heavy-duty)
Perfume
Pillowcase
Play dough in two colors
Play money
Poster board
Powdered sugar
Rock

Rope
Salt
Sod (small piece)
Soft, stackable items
Small treats
Star stickers
Sugar
Sun visor
Suntan lotion
Teddy bear
Teddy bear cookies
Tennis ball
Tissue paper—red, orange, yellow
Tools (small)
Tray
Votive candle (white)
Watch with a second hand
Waxed paper
White rice
Winter clothing
Yarn

Introduction

We're so glad that you've picked the FUNstuff *Ifs, Ands, & Buts Children's Sermons* to use with your children. For many of us, children's sermons were a gift given to us years ago by a loving pastor or teacher. How we marveled at the cleverness of the talk and how it tied so wonderfully with the Bible story or Scripture. Wonderful, too, how God's Word stayed alive in our thoughts long after the sermon was over. We're happy to pass along this wonderful tradition and tool for you to use.

Whether you're new to children's ministry or a seasoned expert, take a minute to read over these tips to make the time with your kids meaningful.

First things first.

• Pray. Pray for the children who will come to hear and learn from you. Pray for positive, receptive spirits to hear God's Word.

• Relax! Being prepared for your talk is your responsibility, but changing children's hearts to love God is not. Leave this soul-changing process to the Holy Spirit.

• Don't try to talk over excited kids. A calm approach and a normal speaking voice will draw your kids to you—and they will quiet down in order to hear you. Establish a gesture or signal up front that will tell them you're ready to begin.

• Have on hand a special rug, mat, or shower curtain for children to sit on during sermon times. This will keep young ones from wiggling too much or straying from the group. Clothesline rope circles also work well. If your sermon spot is a permanent place, use electrical tape in rainbow colors. Remember, if you don't want the kids to move, then be sure that you do.

• Practice beforehand holding props and speaking at the same time.

• Will you find yourself speaking to children in a wide age range? Aim for the middle age and adjust your vocabulary and methods to suit that group. The others will follow.

• Make sure your audience can see you. Who doesn't remember the frustration of trying to see a poorly positioned puppet or felt board?

• There is a difference between "entertaining kids" and keeping them connected and interested. You are more important than the puppet, gizmo, or prop you brought with you. It is **you** and the time you spend with children that will draw a child to Christ.

• Don't feel you need to have all the answers to on-the-spot questions about the Bible. Your promise to find out the answer and connect later will bond with young, eager minds. Just be sure that you follow up.

• Lastly, remember children of all ages learn best with their senses: touching, tasting, hearing, seeing and smelling. When giving a sermon talk, take advantage of all five.

Shadrach, Meshach, and Abednego said, "**If** we are thrown into the furnace…." Jesus said, "I am the way **and** the truth **and** the life…." Gideon said, "**But** LORD…." *Ifs, Ands, & Buts Children's Sermons* takes a look at tiny words on which the meaning of a story may turn. They ask children to suppose, to imagine, to compare and contrast—in creative ways that will keep the whole congregation curious about what you'll do next.

Every sermon has a Bible truth, a key verse, and a Godprint. Not sure what a Godprint is? Check out the explanations beginning on page 107 of the key character traits that God wants to give your kids. A simple format of **On Your Mark**, **Get Set**, **Go** tells you everything you need to get started.

You're off! May God bless you and all that you do for the young-at-heart in his kingdom.

Mary Grace Becker
Susan Martins Miller

Children and the Word of God

There's nothing better than a great story.
Libraries and bookstores bustle with people looking for a good read, or even a movie with an engrossing plot.

Every life is a story waiting to be told. We tell co-workers the stories of our weekends. At times of testimony, we share the hardest conflicts of our personal stories. And we involve children in stories very early. At the dinner table we listen to children tell stories about their day. At bedtime, we read children stories. Looking at photo albums, we share the stories of our families.

God has told his story in his Word. We don't have to wait for children to grow up before they can be captivated by this story. The fundamental story of God's love for his people, his sacrifice so we can know him, and the new lives he wants us to lead are for all ages.

God's plan for children's spiritual development encompasses a community of faith. We see this commanded and demonstrated in the books of the Law through the rituals and festivals of the people of Israel. The very life of the Jewish family and community centered around sharing and celebrating with rich sensory experiences the great stories of faith and God's ongoing presence in their midst.

It's possible for a child to absorb a great deal of information about the Bible without learning to know the person of God and choosing to walk in his steps. But what we really want to teach children is who God is as well as what he has said. As we discover who God is, we see his character revealed in Scripture, in creation, in relationships within a Christian community, and ultimately within ourselves. And we want the same thing for our children.

We want them to be lifelong disciples, not walking Bible encyclopedias. So how do we do this?

The growing child's picture of God is reshaped and transformed by increased understanding and experience. Play is the work of children. We embrace imagination, the power of forming images of reality in our minds, as a gift of God and a key factor in children's development. Imagination plays a role as children stretch to understand the stories of the Bible and God's involvement in their lives. In the children's sermons in this book, you'll find lots of opportunities to let children stretch their imaginations and know God better because they did.

Moral development in children is more than instruction about what is right and wrong. Children need to see moral reasoning in action in the lives of the adults around them. In these children's sermons, you'll be challenged to share pieces of your story so children can see God at work in your life.

Worship is central to spiritual formation. Young children can meet God in authentic ways, although this may not look the same as an adult's encounter with God. These children's sermons will help children encounter God on their own level, with their own words, and respond with awe and wonder at the greatness of God.

God is at work in our lives, directing each story, bringing together intersecting plot lines in our relationships with others. God leaves his imprint on our lives and helps us to pass that imprint on to others. When God is at work in circumstances, in individual lives, and in the faith community, we can see that "God was here." And we rejoice.

Growing into Faith

On the journey of faith development, children pass through various stages. The process of maturing spiritually is not separate from all the other ways kids grow up; it's all part of the same package. When we keep in mind what is going on in the hearts and minds of children, we do a better job of reaching them with God's Word.

The children's sermons in this book are aimed at mixed ages. If you have a more tightly limited age range, you can adapt accordingly. Little ones may need more time to process questions and respond. Older ones may need more opportunity for dialogue and expression of their own opinions. Either way, you don't know what they might say next, so you're always on your toes!

Preschoolers see the world as a very big place. Don't be a giant! Sit with them so you can look them in the eye. They are curious and observant. What looks ordinary to us is full of wonder for a young child. Young children love to use their senses: sight, sound, touch, taste, smell. This is their favorite way to learn. And don't forget their imaginations. Preschoolers love to pretend.

Mentally, preschoolers

- have short attention spans
- ask many questions
- are learning language rapidly
- fear the unfamiliar
- feel important when you ask them to help
- learn through their senses
- have active imaginations
- are curious
- think concretely
- have intense emotions

Socially, preschoolers

- are self-centered
- are learning to take turns
- like to try new things
- will laugh one minute, cry the next

Physically, preschoolers

- are active, love to run and jump
- are developing their large muscles
- are comfortable on the floor
- have boundless energy
- are growing rapidly
- are developing fine motor skills

Spiritually, preschoolers

- can understand that Jesus loves them
- are filled with wonder
- love to read Bible stories
- can experience worship

Younger elementary children really believe the other sex has cooties! They're beginning to find out who they are and what they like, growing in independence every day. They also love to help. Helping you or any other person in authority gives them a huge boost of self-confidence. Remember that kids this age are active, active, active. Don't expect them to sit still for more than five minutes. Provide some activity for them to be involved. Make every moment of your children's sermon count.

Mentally, younger elementary kids

- live in the present
- learn best from creative activities
- love to explore and investigate
- think concretely
- are growing phenomenally in language skills

Socially, younger elementary kids

- love to have a best friend
- mimic the adults in their lives
- are especially loyal to teachers
- have developed a sense of right and wrong
- enjoy working in groups

Physically, younger elementary kids

- are growing slowly, sporadically
- have bursts of energy
- have trouble sitting still
- tire easily

Spiritually, younger elementary kids

- enjoy learning at church
- are open to learning about God
- find it difficult to express feelings
- pray easily if encouraged

Older elementary children learn to see God everywhere. They understand that God is real, eternal, and supremely powerful, and they learn through experience how to reconcile with others. Reality is a good teacher. Kids this age come to see themselves as imperfect people in an imperfect world, and understand their need for God's grace in their lives.

Mentally, older elementary kids

- are curious, ask lots of questions
- love to reason and discuss
- begin to develop longer attention spans
- can memorize and recite
- are developing self-confidence
- can think abstractly
- have a more mature sense of time and space
- are aware that adults are not always right
- want to make their own decisions

Physically, older elementary kids

- grow steadily
- enjoy being active
- want to participate rather than watch
- mature at different rates
- are noisy and love to compete
- become aware of the opposite sex

Socially, older elementary kids

- learn better ways to make and keep friends
- are interested in cultures around the world
- have strong feelings about right and wrong
- need to belong to a peer group
- are becoming more responsible and dependable

Spiritually, older elementary kids

- begin to ask questions about faith
- evaluate different points of view
- enjoy participating in worship
- can apply Christian truth to their own behavior
- like to share and participate in church activities
- can express spiritual thoughts

Ifs

Hot and Cold

On Your Mark

Bible Truth: God wants us to know him.
Bible Verse: But **if** from there you seek the LORD your God, you will find him **if** you look for him with all your heart and with all your soul (Deut. 4:29).
Godprint: Faith

Get Set

You'll need a red ball or other brightly colored small object. Mark Deuteronomy 4:29 in a Bible. Ahead of time, hide the ball among the flowers or furniture at the front of the sanctuary. Don't make it too obvious.

GO!

Everyone cover your eyes with your hands. No peeking! You can't see me now, but do you think I'm still here? *(Yes, of course.)* **What if you couldn't hear my voice? Would you still know that I'm here? Let's try that. I'll be really quiet, and if you think I'm still here, raise one hand— but keep your eyes squeezed shut.**

Pause for about 15 seconds of silence. It will seem like a long time, but don't cut it short. Make some rustling noises as if you might be moving away from the children.

You can open your eyes now. How many of you thought I was still here even though you couldn't see me? I saw a few hands.

- **If I wasn't here and you wanted to find me, what would you do?** *(Look. Call out.)*
- **If you still couldn't find me, what would you do?** *(Keep looking. Or give up.)*
- **Can you think of some things you lose and have to look for?** *(Homework, shoes, toys.)*

Let's do a little looking for something I've lost. I know I had my red ball (or other object) **earlier, but I don't know what I did with it. Maybe you can help me find it. Why don't some of you go over there** (point in one direction) **and the rest of you go over there** (point in another direction). If you have a lot of kids, you might want to make more than two groups.

Encourage the kids to move away from you in their search.

Have you found it yet? No? Well, maybe you're not looking hard enough. Look harder! Harder!

Oh! I have a feeling that (name of child closest to the hidden object) **might be getting close. I'm starting to remember. Yes, I think it's over here somewhere. Warmer! Warmer!**

Play the familiar "hot and cold" game to nudge kids toward where you have hidden the ball. When someone finds the ball, express exuberant thanks and ask the kids to sit down again.

The Bible has something to say about looking really hard. It tells us to look for God really hard! Let's read a verse about that. Ask a volunteer to read Deuteronomy 4:29 in the Bible where you've marked it.

> **But if from there you seek the LORD your God, you will find him if you look for him with all your heart and with all your soul.**

- **What do you think this verse means when it says "If from there"?** (*Wherever we are, we can look for God.*)
- **How does this verse tell us to look for God?** (*With all our heart and soul.*)
- **What do you think it means to look for God with all your heart and all your soul?**

God knew that the people he loved might sometimes forget about that love. They would wander away from him and think that other things were more important than God. But he wanted them to know that if that happened, they could still come back to him. A very important word in this verse is a very small word—if. *If* we seek God, and *if* we look for him with all our hearts, we will find him.

The next time you lose something and you're looking really hard for it, maybe you'll remember this verse and remember to look for God with all your heart and all your soul! God wants us to know him, so he's always there when we look for him.

Bow for prayer. **Dear God, thank you that no matter where we go and no matter what we think is important, you want us to know you. Thank you for not hiding from us, but always being there when we look for you. Amen.**

Stick 'em Ups

On Your Mark

Bible Truth: God wants us to pray with humility.

Bible Verse: If my people, who are called by my name, will humble themselves and pray and seek my face and turn from their wicked ways, then will I hear from heaven and will forgive their sin and will heal their land (2 Chron. 7:14).

Godprint: Prayerfulness

Get Set

You'll need a glass jar filled with white rice leaving a 1-inch gap at the top, a box of small teddy bear cookies, small sturdy table. Mark 2 Chronicles 7:14 in a Bible.

GO!

Twist the cover securely on the jar, shake it, and hold it high for your children to see. Have the box of cookies close by. **When we sin or do wrong we often try and hide it from ourselves. We play hide-and-go-seek—but wish to stay hidden! We also try and hide it from others. We think if we somehow hide our sin, it can't be seen.**

• **Name a wrong that children your age try and cover up.** *(Lying, stealing, cheating, disobedience.)*

Each time a child mentions a wrong, ask him or her to come up and take a bear cookie and push it into the rice-filled jar until it is completely covered.

Hold the jar up for the group to see. **We may fool ourselves into thinking that our sins are "out of sight, out of mind" but God knows our faults. Even if we're successful in hiding things from ourselves, nothing is hidden from him.**

Place the jar on the table and open your Bible to 2 Chronicles 7:14. Read the verse yourself or have a confident reader do so.

If my people, who are called by my name, will humble themselves and pray and seek my face and turn from their wicked ways, then will I hear from heaven and will forgive their sin and will heal their land.

In this Old Testament verse from 2 Chronicles, the king of Israel, wise and great King Solomon, asks God a question. What must his people do when they sin? God actually appears to Solomon and tells him one-on-one. Ask the kids to repeat God's instructions after you.

• **Be humble and stop doing wrong.** (Pause for children to repeat.)
• **Pray.** (Pause for children to repeat.)
• **Look for God in everything you do.** (Pause for children to repeat.)

We, like the Israelites, must do these things too. God promises that when we do, he'll hear and answer our prayers. Remember, God is listening.

• **What does it mean to be humble?** *(To be modest, not a braggart, not insist that our way is the only way to go.)*
• **How can prayer bring you closer to God?** *(We learn to recognize his voice and to do what he asks.)*
• **Is God with you throughout the day? Does he take a break? Why do you think he chooses to stay with us even when we're sleeping at night?**

Hand the jar to a volunteer from your group and ask him or her to place it on the table. **Christine, gently shake the jar from side to side. Be sure not to lift the jar, just leave it on the table while you "shake and stir" from side to side. Do this until we see at least one of the bear cookies rise to the surface. Let it remind all of us to bring our wrongs up and out into the mercy of God's forgiveness.** Each time a figure "pops up" remove it from the jar.

Distribute extra cookies to your hungry listeners.

The Time Is Now

Bible Truth: God gives us courage to do hard things.

Bible Verse: For **if** you remain silent at this time, relief and deliverance for the Jews will arise from another place, but you and your father's family will perish. And who knows but that you have come to royal position for such a time as this? (Esth. 4:14).

Godprint: Courage

Get Set

You'll need a large bag or box filled with something you can safely stack—large soft blocks, boxes of food, boxes of tissue, or rolls of paper towels. Mark Esther 4:14 in a Bible.

GO!

As kids gather, put your finger to your lips and say "Shh." Keep doing this until everyone has settled down quietly. Then whisper as you continue to talk.

You're doing a great job at being silent. Let's see if you can be silent no matter what. Remember, shhh.

Start digging around in your bag or box while kids are being quiet. **Let's see, I've got some things in here that I need to take care of while you sit there silently. Shh! I'm just going to stack these things right here and see if I can keep it all organized.** Pull items out of the box or bag and stack them as high and precariously as you can. Make sure no one will get hurt if they fall. As the tower gets more dramatic, keep on stacking. Make sure the pile is wobbly enough to make the kids a little nervous. **I've been carrying these things around all day because I wasn't sure what to do with them. What do you think I should do?** At this point some of the kids may be ready to break the code of silence, either to answer your question, to warn you not to stack any higher, or to give you advice. If you'd like, you can let the pile safely topple.

• **How many of you wanted to talk so you could tell me what you thought about my stack?**

• **How many of you wanted to stay silent because that's what I asked you to do?**

The Bible tells a story about a young woman who had to make a decision about whether to talk or to remain silent. This young woman was Esther. Can anyone help me tell her story? *(Esther was a Jewish woman married to the king of Persia. Enemies of the Jews tricked the king into signing a law that would allow them to kill Jewish people on a certain day. The king did not know Esther was Jewish. She was afraid to tell him, but she knew she was the only person who could help her people.)*

Let's read one important verse from this story and find out what Esther's cousin, Mordecai, said to her. Ask a volunteer to read Esther 4:14.

> For if you remain silent at this time, relief and deliverance for the Jews will arise from another place, but you and your father's family will perish. And who knows but that you have come to royal position for such a time as this?

- What would happen if Esther was silent? *(God would help his people another way.)*
- Mordecai thinks that Esther may have become queen for a special reason. What might it be? *(To help the Jewish people when no one else could.)*

There were a lot of "ifs" in Esther's decision. If she kept silent, what would happen? *(Her people could be killed.)* If she spoke up, what would happen? *(She could make the king angry and be killed herself.)*

Mordecai thought that God had allowed Esther to become the queen just so she could help when her people needed help the most. Do you remember what Esther did? *(She risked her life and went to the king. He made a new law that the Jewish people could fight back. Esther saved her people.)* Esther believed that God would give her courage to do something hard.

Sometimes we have to do something hard. We think, "If I do this, what will happen? If I don't do this, what will happen?" Esther answered the big "if" question with courage because she knew she had God's help. The great thing is that we have God's help with hard things too. Let's thank him for that.

Bow for prayer. **God, when Esther faced a big "if," you helped her make the courageous choice because she knew you would help her. Thank you for giving us the courage to do the hard things you want us to do. In Jesus' name, amen.**

Doo-dads

On Your Mark

Bible Truth: God is with us wherever we go.
Bible Verse: **If** I go up to the heavens, you are there; **if** I make my bed in the depths, you are there. **If** I rise on the wings of the dawn, **if** I settle on the far side of the sea… (Ps. 139:8–9).
Godprint: Preciousness

Get Set

You'll need cotton balls, vanilla, butterscotch, peppermint, lemon or spearmint extracts, and bottles of a favorite "heavenly" and sea-breezy perfume or cologne. Mark Psalm 139:8-9 in a Bible.

GO!

Fathers, uncles, and granddads help us in many ways. We think of them often, especially when we want something fixed or need a strong helping hand.

• How do men in your family help you? What about neighbors, teachers, or coaches?

Wherever we go, God, our heavenly Father, comes along too. God is everywhere. Like the sweet smell of the grass after a warm summer rain, or the cold, crisp air of a bright autumn day, or the smell of Christmas snow, God is very, very near.

• What is your favorite smell?
• If the word "help" was a smell, what smell would it be?

Distribute scented cotton balls to your group. **Smell the sweetness of your cotton ball.** Pause. **Mmm. That smells grand! Next time you need a reminder that God, our helper, is close, take a sniff of your favorite scent. It can be the perfume of a sweet rose or the smell of fresh baked bread. Let it remind you that God is as close to you as the air you breathe. In fact, he's closer. Because we are precious and valuable to God, he will stay close to Jenny and Steven, Paul and Christine.** (If time allows, name all the children in your group.)

Open your Bible and read today's Scripture, Psalm 139:8–9.

If I go up to the heavens, you are there; if I make my bed in the depths, you are there. If I rise on the wings of the dawn, if I settle on the far side of the sea . . . .

The first part of today's verse states, *"If I go up to the heavens, you are there."*

• Not too high, please! When sitting on a swing or flying in an airplane do you imagine yourself being close to God in heaven? What do you think heaven smells like?
• Is it a comfort to know whether you're swimming in the ocean or flying in a plane God is there with you? What if you were to skip from star to star in a moon-bright sky?

Distribute new cotton balls spritzed with a heavenly scent.

The next part of the verse states, *"If I make my bed in the depths, you are there."* Deep at the bottom of the ocean live many creatures. Most have no eyesight. Sunlight cannot penetrate the miles and miles of water below the sea's surface. Deep-sea creatures learn to live in darkness. Even if we were to find ourselves living at the bottom of the deep, dark sea, God's Word tells us he is there also.
Distribute fresh cotton balls spritzed with an ocean scent.

Share a time when children want to hide from God. **How can you remember the love of God during such times? Why is it so important that we tell others about the love and preciousness of God?**

The last part of our verse reads, *"If I rise on the wings of the dawn, if I settle on the far side of the sea…"*

• Tell me in your own words what the final part of today's Scripture means to you.
• Can we be far away from God—and yet never leave home? Why or why not?

If you choose, distribute a final scent.

Praise God that he considers us more precious than expensive perfume. He is like the best dad, uncle, grandpa, and coach all wrapped up into one! May we always be blessed by his sweet, mysterious, and holy presence.

Fire of Faith

On Your Mark

Bible Truth: God wants us to stand firm in our faith.

Bible Verses: **If** we are thrown into the blazing furnace, the God we serve is able to save us from it, and he will rescue us from your hand, O king. But even **if** he does not, we want you to know, O king, that we will not serve your gods or worship the image of gold you have set up (Dan. 3:17–18).

Godprint: Conviction

Get Set

You'll need red, orange, or yellow tissue paper and some large marshmallows. Mark Daniel 3:17–18 in a Bible.

GO!

As kids gather, have them help you scrunch up the tissue paper and make a blazing paper fire. Gather close around it.

That is one hot fire, let me tell you. I think maybe we should all back up a little bit. We don't want to get scorched. Pause to have the kids scoot away from the fire.

I thought it would be better back here, but it's still too hot for me. Let's scoot back some more. Pause to have kids scoot back further.

Ah, much better. Do you ever sit around a campfire and throw stuff into it? Maybe little bits of wood or some small rocks. I like to sit and watch the little things I throw burn up in the fire. Let's toss something into our imaginary fire. Pass out marshmallows and let everyone toss one into the fire. If you'd like, you can let kids snack on marshmallows as you continue.

A roaring hot fire like this one makes me think of a Bible story. Can you guess which one? *(Shadrach, Meshach, and Abednego in the fiery furnace.)*

• **Do you remember how that story started?** *(The king wanted everyone to bow down to a huge gold statue, but Shadrach, Meshach, and Abednego would not do it.)*
The king found out about these three guys and ordered them to come and see him. He

said something like, "You'd better bow down to my statue or else I'll throw you into a blazing hot furnace. What god will be able to help you then?" Let's look in the Book of Daniel to find out what the three young men said. Ask a volunteer to read Daniel 3:17–18.

> If we are thrown into the blazing furnace, the God we serve is able to save us from it, and he will rescue us from your hand, O king. But even if he does not, we want you to know, O king, that we will not serve your gods or worship the image of gold you have set up.

I see two little "if" words in those verses that help us understand what they mean.

- What is the first "if"? (If we are thrown into the blazing furnace...)
- What do Shadrach, Meshach, and Abednego believe God can do if that happens? (Save them; rescue them from the king.)
- What is the second "if?" (Even if he does not...)
- What do Shadrach, Meshach, and Abednego say about that? (They still will not bow down to the statue.)

Well, the king didn't like that attitude at all. He heated up the furnace seven times hotter than it usually was. Then he threw them into the furnace. But they didn't burn up! They weren't even a little bit burned. When they came out of the fire safe and sound, even the king believed in the true God.

Sometimes things happen to us that make us feel like we're in a fiery furnace and there's just no way out. Shadrach, Meshach, and Abednego help us remember that God is with us, no matter what. They stood firm in their faith in the one true God. Now that's a fire of faith!

Bow for prayer. Lord, thank you for being such a great God. Help us to stand firm in our faith, no matter what happens to us. We want to worship only you. Amen.

I Double Dog Dare You

On Your Mark

Bible Truth: Remembering what God says helps us to obey him.

Bible Verses: Then Jesus was led by the Spirit into the desert to be tempted by the devil. After fasting forty days and forty nights, he was hungry. The tempter came to him and said, "**If** you are the Son of God, tell these stones to become bread." Jesus answered, "It is written: 'Man does not live on bread alone, but on every word that comes from the mouth of God.'" Then the devil took him to the holy city and had him stand on the highest point of the temple. "**If** you are the Son of God," he said, "throw yourself down. For it is written: 'He will command his angels concerning you and they will lift you up in their hands, so that you will not strike your foot against a stone.'" Jesus answered him, "It is also written: 'Do not put the Lord your God to the test.' " Again, the devil took him to a very high mountain and showed him all the kingdoms of the world and their splendor. "All this I will give you," he said, "**if** you will bow down and worship me." Jesus said to him, "Away from me, Satan! For it is written: 'Worship the Lord your God, and serve him only.'" Then the devil left him, and angels came and attended him (Matt. 4:1–11).

Godprint: Obedience

Get Set

You'll need a bag of small treats, enough for all the kids, and a watch with a second hand. Mark Matthew 4 in a Bible. Optional: chocolate cake, $50 bill.

GO!

As kids gather, make sure they see your bag of treats. **I would guess that some of you would like one of these treats. Right? I'll tell you what. If you can keep absolutely quiet and still for 15 seconds, I'll give you one of these. Ready? Go.** Let a full 15 seconds pass, then distribute the treats.

What if I had a nice big chocolate cake and I said I would give the whole cake to you, to eat all by yourself. If you cheat on your next spelling test to get 100 percent, the cake is yours. Pause for reactions.

Or what if I said I had a nice, new, crisp $50 bill to give you if you get a can of paint and paint your name in the carpet right here in the church. What do you think about that?

Pause for responses.

Can anyone think of a word that describes what I just did? Pause. **I tempted you. I made you think about doing something you knew was wrong so you could get something you wanted.**

Show your Bible open to Matthew 4. (If you have enough time, ask a volunteer to read Matthew 4:1–11.) **In Matthew 4, the Bible tells us that the devil tempted Jesus. Jesus had not eaten anything in 40 days. He was hungry! Can anyone tell us how the devil tempted Jesus?** *(He tempted him to use his supernatural power to turn stones to bread, vs. 3; he tempted him to use angels and a miracle to save himself from falling, vss. 5-6; he tempted him with power and a kingdom, vss. 8-9.)*

The devil said, "If you…" and tempted Jesus with some things that looked pretty good. That little word "if" is pretty important when we talk about temptation. Jesus could easily have done the things the devil wanted him to do. But he didn't. Who remembers how Jesus responded to temptation? *(He relied on the Word of God. He told Satan what God's Word said about why the temptations were wrong, vss. 4, 7, 10.)*

We face temptations every day. Maybe you're tempted to cheat on your homework, or tell your mom you did your chores when you didn't, or watch TV when your dad told you not to.

Jesus knows what temptation feels like. He knows how easy it would be to do those things. But he also shows us how we can keep from doing the wrong things we're tempted to do. He remembered what God said, and we can too. Remember what God says about lying or cheating or stealing.

Bow for prayer. **Dear God, thank you that you tell us what is right and wrong. Thank you for showing us the way out of the temptation trap. Help us to depend on you when we're tempted to do something we shouldn't. In your Son's name, amen.**

"What If?"

On Your Mark

Bible Truth: God wants us to make an extra effort for friendship, even with people we don't like.
Bible Verses: You have heard that it was said, "Eye for eye, and tooth for tooth." But I tell you, Do not resist an evil person. **If** someone strikes you on the right cheek, turn to him the other also. And **if** someone wants to sue you and take your tunic, let him have your cloak as well. **If** someone forces you to go one mile, go with him two miles (Matt. 5:38–41).
Godprint: Friendliness

Get Set

Mark Matthew 5:38–41 in a Bible.

GO!

Let's play an imagination game today. The game is called "What if?" I'll start. **What if...you opened your refrigerator at home to find a tuna fish sandwich dancing with a slice of cheddar cheese?** Your children will smile to think of such a surprise!

• **Who else can come up with a "what if?" Please remember to make it fun and not too silly.**

Now, the "What if?" game works both ways. By that I mean that it can be hard to do, as well as fun to imagine. Let me show you. Please stand! Instruct your kids to walk in a circle around you. Nice and slow will do just fine. Now, I will mention some new "What if?" situations and as you're walking I want you to pantomime or act out what you hear.

What if...I gave you a pillow to hold? Show me what holding a real pillow would look like. Pause as your children perform the action.

Good! What if...I gave you a very heavy book to hold? Show me what that would look like. Pause.

What if...I gave you a very heavy bag of gold to hold. Show me what that would look like.

Finally, **what if…I gave you 25 concrete bricks to hold? Show me!** Ask kids to stop and give themselves a round of applause for a job well done before returning to their spots. **Good job, everyone. Let's put on our listening ears and hear today's Bible verse.** Open your Bible to Matthew 5:38–41 and read today's verse.

> You have heard that it was said, "Eye for eye, and tooth for tooth." But I tell you, Do not resist an evil person. If someone strikes you on the right cheek, turn to him the other also. And if someone wants to sue you and take your tunic, let him have your cloak as well. If someone forces you to go one mile, go with him two miles.

- **What if** someone hurt your feelings on purpose? What might be your response? **What if** they did it again?
- What do you think Jesus is trying to tell us in this Scripture verse?

This is hard. **What if** someone you know mistreats you, takes something from you, or calls you names behind your back? For many of us our reaction would not be as Jesus would want. Friendships that may start off wonderful and fun don't always stay that way. The attitudes and behaviors of others can get pretty heavy.

Remember, Jesus loves us and does not want us to be hurt. His message for us today, however, is to make the effort and choice to love others and act with a generous heart—rather than choosing to be unforgiving or spiteful. All people, even those who hurt us, are part of the family of Christ. So when things get heavy, put on the attitude of Christ. He promises he will help us to make the right choice.

Cheer-ah Pet

On Your Mark

Bible Truth: God cares for us and gives us what we need.

Bible Verses: And why do you worry about clothes? See how the lilies of the field grow. They do not labor or spin. Yet I tell you that not even Solomon in all his splendor was dressed like one of these. **If that is how God clothes the grass of the field, which is here today and tomorrow is thrown into the fire, will he not much more clothe you, O you of little faith?** (Matt. 6:28–30).

Godprint: Trust

Get Set

You'll need sod (grass rolls), old knife or sod cutter. Optional: cotton balls, small pom-poms or 2-inch polystyrene balls, large wiggle eyes found at craft stores, glue. Mark Matthew 6:28–30 in a Bible.

Use strips of sod to make little furry grass creatures (think caterpillars or small hedgehogs!) for a terrific outdoor spring or summer sermon activity. Plan beforehand whether you'd like to make just one creature to use in your talk or if you would prefer for each child to have his or her own creature. For added appeal, glue wiggle eyes to the center of two cotton balls, pom-poms, or small polystyrene balls. Wedge eyes into the grass at the head of each strip.

GO!

Before meeting with your kids, unroll the fresh sod strips and cut into equal vertical pieces. Shake out the loose dirt from one. Add eyes, if you'd like.

Drape the fuzzy green grass creature over your shoulder. **On such a beautiful day, it's great to be outdoors! And look, I brought a friend with me. Her name is Polly.** Pet Polly.

- **Which season is your favorite time of year?**
- **What other creepy-crawly, furry, or winged creatures remind you of springtime?**

Our Bible verse today is from the book of Matthew. Hand your Bible to a confident reader and ask him or her to read Matthew 6:28–30.

And why do you worry about clothes? See how the lilies of the field grow. They do

not labor or spin. Yet I tell you that not even Solomon in all his splendor was dressed like one of these. If that is how God clothes the grass of the field, which is here today and tomorrow is thrown into the fire, will he not much more clothe you, O you of little faith?

God has wisdom to share in today's Bible verses. To sum it up nicely will take just two words. Anyone care to guess what they are? *Pause as children tell you what they think.* **Good for you! The two words are *stop worrying!* We spend a lot of time worrying about things that we have no control over or just aren't as important as we make them out to be. Let's see, I can think of a few kid worries: *Will the school bus be late this morning? I'm worried about the big test tomorrow.* And how about the famous, *I have nothing to wear* worry!**

· **What things do you worry about? What about your parents?**
· **What does God tell us in today's Bible verses about worry?** *(Trust in him to care for you.)*

Take Polly off your shoulder and drape her over your arm or knee. **God tells us that he "clothes the grass of the field" and gives the flowers their loveliness. Solomon, the king mentioned in today's verses, was the third king of Israel. He was well-known in Old Testament times for his beautiful clothes and great wealth.**

Jesus tells us it's foolish to worry about our clothes, because he knows what we need. Stop worrying! Look at how he cares for the simple things of nature that are here for a summer day and gone tomorrow. It's a good thing that Polly here doesn't rely on me for sunshine or rain.

How much more will Jesus will care for us, people made in his own image? So much more! Let's give a cheer for Jesus. *Ask kids to shout, Hip, Hip, Hooray, for Jesus!* **Oh, I think we can do better than that.** *Have kids try again.* **Much better! Remember, God sent his only Son, Jesus, to die on the cross—not for the grass or the beautiful flowers of the world, but for his sons and daughters—that's you and me.**

If you wish, have kids pick up their own grass strips, shake out the loose dirt, and add eyes. Suggest that once they get home they put their grassy "pet" into a shallow tray of water to keep its fur thick and green!

Rockin' Rocks

On Your Mark

Bible Truth: God is worthy of our praise.
Bible Verse: "I tell you," he replied, "**if** they keep quiet, the stones will cry out" (Luke 19:40).
Godprint: Worship

Get Set

You'll need some packing peanuts in a bowl or sheets of bubble wrap and 8 to 10 rocks. Mark Luke 19:40 in a Bible.

GO!

Have you ever been lying in your bed on a hot summer night with the window open, and you just wish all those rocks outside would keep quiet? They can sure be talkative! No? You don't think so? Mmm. Let's listen to these rocks for a moment.

Set out several large rocks in the center of your circle and ask everyone to be perfectly quiet so you can hear the rocks. Cock your head as if to listen carefully. **Do you hear that? I can hear that they're trying to say something, but I can't quite make out the words. Can anyone help me? Tell me what the rocks are saying.**

Pause to see if any kids will respond. You might get some funny looks—or some imaginative answers! **Mmm. Maybe we need some more rocks so they'll be a little louder.** Add more rocks to the pile and listen again. **These modern rocks are just not as talkative as they used to be.**

Did you know Jesus talked about noisy rocks? It was on the day that he rode into Jerusalem on a donkey and all the people cheered for him as a king. Let's hear you cheer for Jesus. Let's say "Hosanna! Blessed is the one who comes in the name of the Lord." Pause and have the kids—or the whole congregation—join you. **"Hosanna! Blessed is the one who comes in the name of the Lord."**

Some of the religious leaders did not like what was happening. They told Jesus that he should scold the people because they were making too much noise. Let's find out what Jesus said. Ask a volunteer to read Luke 19:40.

"I tell you," he replied, "if they keep quiet, the stones will cry out."

• What do you suppose Jesus meant when he said the stones would cry out?

If the people didn't praise God, then the stones would! Jesus meant that God is worthy of our praise, and nothing can stop his creation from praising him. I think it's great that people—you and I—get to praise God.

• Name some ways that we praise God.
• What's your favorite way to praise God?

Today we're going to praise God in a way that reminds us of what Jesus said about the stones. Pass out the bubble wrap or set a bowl of packing peanuts where everyone can take some. Kids can pop the bubble wrap or snap packing peanuts in half to make the sound of popping rocks. Whenever you "pop a rock," say, "I praise Jesus for_____" and fill in the blank. We'll all do it at one time to really rock with praise. Ready? Go!

Optional: You may want to invite the entire congregation to participate in rockin' praise.

Close with prayer. God, we want to praise you right along with the rocks. No one deserves our praise more than you do. Thank you for creating us so we can praise you. Amen.

Leading a Child to Christ

A child's belief system develops from several bases including relationships, personal experience, and knowledge. As kids discover the person of God, they'll grow into a position where they're ready to allow God to enter their lives with his transforming power. As you learn to know and love the children you minister to, you may find them ready to make a commitment to Christ. How will you lead them in this important step of faith?

Though it may seem a strange place to start, think of a sunset. God orchestrates all the elements of the atmosphere, geography, and weather to create a skyscape that swells to a point of perfect beauty, then fades quickly and is gone.

On a spiritual level, God orchestrates all the elements of a child's life to create a teachable moment when hunger for God comes to the forefront. Those moments are as precious and fleeting as a sunset. A discerning teacher senses when the Holy Spirit has prepared a child's heart, offers the simple truth of the Gospel, and allows a child to respond.

If you sense that a child is ready to open his or her life to God, speak simply and directly. Do you know how much God loves you, Eric? Do you know that God wants to make you his special child and welcome you into his family?

Use these Scriptures to explain God's plan of salvation. You may want to read them from the Bible, or explain the truth in children's language.

> **Psalm 139:13-16—God loved you even before you were born. He knows all about you and has a wonderful plan for your life.**
>
> **1 John 1:9-10—No one is perfect enough for God. We all sin and mess up.**
>
> **John 3:16—God sent Jesus to pay for the sins of the whole world—including yours! Jesus wants to be your Savior. Would you like to pray to accept him?**
>
> **1 John 3:1—God has given you a wonderful gift—he's made you his child!**

Children approach God with very different levels of spiritual maturity and understanding. Their first expression of faith won't make them theological experts! Faith development is a lifelong process. Encourage children to open their lives to God's love and transforming power. Remember, every step toward God is a good one.

This is so that you'll live in deep reverence before GOD lifelong, observing all his rules and regulations that I'm commanding you, you and your children and your grandchildren, living good long lives. Listen obediently, Israel. Do what you're told so that you'll have a good life, a life of abundance and bounty, just as GOD promised, in a land abounding in milk and honey. Attention, Israel! GOD, our God! GOD the one and only! Love GOD, your God, with your whole heart: love him with all that's in you, love him with all you've got! Write these commandments that I've given you today on your hearts. Get them inside of you and then get them inside your children. Talk about them wherever you are, sitting at home or walking in the street; talk about them from the time you get up in the morning to when you fall into bed at night. Tie them on your hands and foreheads as a reminder; inscribe them on the doorposts of your homes and on your city gates.

Deuteronomy 6:2–9 *The Message*

Let these children alone. Don't get between them and me. These children are the kingdom's pride and joy.

Luke 18:16 *The Message*

Phone-y Charges

On Your Mark

Bible Truth: God wants us to do his will even when it's hard.
Bible Verse: Father, **if** you are willing, take this cup from me; yet not my will, but yours be done (Luke 22:42).
Godprint: Submissiveness

Get Set

You'll need a cellular phone with the sound turned off. Optional: small orange that fits firmly in a cup, box of toothpicks. Mark Luke 22:42 in a Bible.

GO!

Hold your cell phone up for your group to see. **It's hard to believe that there was ever a time we didn't have cell phones. In the past, if a car broke down, or a loved one was late getting home from a party, families worried—yet hoped—they'd soon hear the car pulling into the driveway. With no way to keep in touch, hope was all families had.** Slip your cell phone into your pocket.

• **Share a time when you were without a phone or a way to contact your parents or sitter. What did that feel like?**
• **How does separation—like getting lost at the zoo—make you feel?**

Hoping for the best is a good thing. But hope in God our Father is far, far better. Today's Scripture verse connects hope (raise one hand) **and prayer** (raise your other hand and join it in prayer with the first) **together into a powerful tool—more powerful than a cell phone with unlimited minutes!—when fear, uneasiness, and the unexpected lie ahead.**

Open your Bible to Luke 22:42 and ask a confident reader to read the verse aloud.

Father, if you are willing, take this cup from me; yet not my will, but yours be done.

The setting of today's Scripture is a garden sprinkled with olive trees. Jesus often went to the Mount of Olives to pray to his Father. Sadly, today's prayer is a troubled one. (If you wish, have your group kneel with you and join hands in prayer as you repeat Luke 22:42.).

The "cup" that today's Scripture mentions is not a real drinking cup. It is a picture word that symbolizes something filled with worry and fear. If you wish, pass out the toothpicks *(beware: toothpicks are choking hazards for very young children)* and hand the cup with the orange to a child closest to you. Take a moment and think of a fear or worry you or someone you care about has, and then pierce the fruit with your toothpick before passing it on.

• What everyday troubles or worries do children experience that make them fretful or nervous?

Jesus is afraid. He knows that he will suffer greatly in the days to come. The only perfect man to ever live on earth, Jesus, will be falsely charged by the Jewish council in Jerusalem, stand trial before the Roman governor, Pilate, whipped, and sentenced to death.

• How many times do you think you can pray to God the Father to help ease your worries and fears? Once, twice, three hundred? Explain your answer.

Jesus pours his heart (hold up the cup) into prayer and then passes the troubles off to his all-knowing Father. Pass the cup around for children to gently feel with the pointy toothpicks. Yet, with his thoughts expressed, Jesus remains steadfast, committed to the will of his Father. His Father's will was that Jesus would die on the cross for our sins.

What have we learned today? Follow Jesus' example and pray when troubles, fear, or worry threaten our inner peace and hope. God will not abandon us. He is with us every step of the way.

I Believe!

On Your Mark

Bible Truth: God uses his great power to save us.
Bible Verse: **If** you confess with your mouth, "Jesus is Lord," and believe in your heart that God raised him from the dead, you will be saved (Rom. 10:9).
Godprint: Faith

Get Set

Mark Romans 10:9 in a Bible.

GO!

I believe purple is the best color of all, don't you? No? What do you believe is the best color? Pause for responses.

I believe that the peacock is the most beautiful animal in the world, don't you? No? What do you believe is the most beautiful animal? Pause for responses.

I believe winter is the best season of the year. All that snow and ice—I love it! How can anyone not love it? We all agree, right? No? Pause for responses.

I believe that roasted red peppers are the best thing in the whole world that you can put on a pizza. Surely you agree? No? Pause for responses.

Mmm. We seem to have a lot of different opinions about these things. Let's see if we can find something that we can agree on. I believe that colored pencils are better than crayons. Surely you agree with me on that. Pause for responses.

We don't seem to be getting anywhere. Let's try again. I believe that the sun comes up every morning. You're not going to argue with me on that one, are you? Pause for responses.

Now we're getting somewhere. I believe that the ocean has salty water. Do we all agree on that? Pause.
On some things, we can all have our own opinions, and no opinion is wrong. And some

things, like the sun rising every day, are facts that no one can argue with.

But on some things, what we say we believe really matters. Let's look at a Bible verse about that. Ask a volunteer to read Romans 10:9.

> If you confess with your mouth, "Jesus is Lord," and believe in your heart that God raised him from the dead, you will be saved.

• What does "confess with your mouth" mean? *(What you say you believe.)*
• What is the most important thing we can say we believe? *(Jesus is Lord.)*
• Why is it also important to believe in your heart?
• What is the first word in this verse. *(If.)*

"If" is a tiny little word, but it makes a huge difference. Jesus died to save us from our sins, and God raised Jesus from the dead. If we have faith in Jesus, God saves us. That's not like a favorite color or a pizza topping. It's something that God wants us to believe in our hearts.

Bow for prayer. **God, thank you for raising Jesus from the dead. We believe in your power. Help us to have faith to say that Jesus is Lord, and help us not to be afraid to say it aloud to other people. We pray in your strength. Amen.**

Johnny on the Spot

On Your Mark

Bible Truth: God wants all of us to use the abilities he gives us.

Bible Verses: **If** the foot should say, "Because I am not a hand, I do not belong to the body," it would not for that reason cease to be part of the body. And **if** the ear should say, "Because I am not an eye, I do not belong to the body," it would not for that reason cease to be part of the body. **If** the whole body were an eye, where would the sense of hearing be? **If** the whole body were an ear, where would the sense of smell be? But in fact God has arranged the parts in the body, every one of them, just as he wanted them to be. **If** they were all one part, where would the body be? As it is, there are many parts, but one body (1 Cor. 12:15–20).

Godprint: Community

Get Set

You'll need three large and colorful poster board circles. Mark 1 Corinthians 12:15–20 in a Bible.

GO!

Place the poster board circles on the floor. Ask early arrivers to please sit and "take their spots."

Today's Scripture is a long one! But that doesn't mean it's difficult to understand. **Who would like to read today's verses, 1 Corinthians 12:15–20, aloud from my Bible?** Pause as the verses are read.

- In your own words, sum up today's Scripture. What do you think the Apostle Paul is trying to teach us with these words?
- Imagine breathing out of your eye and seeing with your ears! How wonderful is our body's design just the way God made it!

We only need to be sick for a day or two to appreciate the magnificence of the human body. We've all tried to breathe out of a stuffy nose. Think about trying to eat when your tummy hurts or taking a ride on a bicycle with a sprained ankle.

In 1 Corinthians 12:15 Paul compares the believers in a church to the human body. Each has a job to do. And like any group of people who work together, a few have great gifts.

Ask a child "on the spot" to stand. **Think of the soloist in the choir. There are few people who could do what she or he does. We may wish with all our hearts to sing high, long, and clear, but it's a gift only a few have.** If you wish, put your volunteer "on the spot" and ask if he or she would join you in singing a few bars of a favorite hymn before sitting down.

Ask the child on spot #2 to rise. **The wonderful sermons by our pastor make many of us wonder how he got to be so smart. To think and talk—all at the same time—takes talent!** Ask your volunteer if he or she would pantomime an enthusiastic pastor delivering a sermon before sitting down.

Finally, ask the child on spot #3 to rise. **And what about the amazing men and women who whip up our delicious church suppers? Mmm. Double chunk, chocolate, and marshmallow brownies drizzled with caramel sauce make my mouth water. How about you?** Ask your volunteer to pantomime removing a brownie tray from the oven—having forgotten to put on an oven mitt!

Our truth for today is this: Try not to dwell jealously on the gifts of others. Everyone has a place in church and in God's kingdom. Just like our bodies it's the way God designed it. Not all the parts can be the head. My, my. Just imagine what *that* body would look like! Use the gifts God has given you and encourage your friends to do the same. If time allows, ask children to share what they are good at (their gifts or talents) with the group before heading back to their seats.

The Big Lie

On Your Mark

Bible Truth: God wants us to walk in the light and live by the truth.

Bible Verses: **If** we claim that we have fellowship with him yet walk in the darkness, we lie and do not live by the truth. But **if** we walk in the light, as he is in the light, we have fellowship with one another, and the blood of Jesus, his Son, purifies us from all sin (1 John 1:6–7).

Godprint: Integrity

Get Set

You'll need a Bible with a bookmark at 1 John 1:6-7.

GO!

As kids gather, give them a big grin and act as if you're very proud of yourself. **Let me tell you about the week I've had. It's been the best week in my whole life. I did more work than anyone else. I read more books than anyone else I know. I fixed some great meals for my family, and when I went shopping, I found all the best deals. My car is the cleanest one in the parking lot, and my yard is the best-looking one in the whole neighborhood.** Continue impressing everyone with all your accomplishments.

Now, tell me what you did this week. Most likely, kids will offer some of their own proud accomplishments—soccer goals, test grades, etc. Congratulate them, especially for the ones you think might be true!

Next week is going to be a big week for exercise. I claim that I already can do 200 sit-ups and 500 jumping jacks every day. So I claim that I can add 300 push-ups every day. In my spare time, I claim that I can read three books every day. What are you going to be doing this week? Coax the kids into making outlandish claims of their own. If you need to encourage participation, ask kids to fill in the blank: "I claim that I can_____." By now you should be getting some wild claims from the kids.

Wow, we're all claiming that we can do some pretty great things. Do you know what? I can't really do 200 sit-ups and 500 jumping jacks. I claimed that I could, but it's not really true. Maybe next week we should get together and find out if we really did any of these things!

How many of our claims do you think would turn out to be true? The kids should start admitting that perhaps not everything they claimed they could do will turn out to be true. If you need to, steer the discussion in that direction by asking the group about some of the specific claims. However, be careful not to embarrass any one child.

The Bible tells us something about making claims that are not true. Let's find out what it is. Ask a volunteer to read 1 John 1:6–7.

> **If we claim that we have fellowship with him yet walk in the darkness, we lie and do not live by the truth. But if we walk in the light, as he is in the light, we have fellowship with one another, and the blood of Jesus, his Son, purifies us from all sin.**

- **According to this verse, what does God want us to do?** *(Walk in the light; live by the truth; have fellowship with one another.)*
- **What kind of false claim does this verse talk about?** *(Lying about having fellowship with God; not really living God's way.)*

This verse uses one little word two times: "if." If we claim to have fellowship with God but we don't act like we do, we're lying. But *if* we walk in God's ways, then God cleans us from all our sin. God wants us to do on the outside what we say we believe on the inside. That's called integrity. And there are no ifs, ands, and buts about that!

Bow for prayer. **Father, you call us to walk in the light and live by the truth. Help us to show in our lives that we want to walk in your ways. Help us to be more like you every day so that we're not making any false claims. In Jesus' name, amen.**

A Glorious Garden

On Your Mark

Bible Truth: We can be sure God forgives us when we've done something wrong.

Bible Verses: **If** we claim to be without sin, we deceive ourselves and the truth is not in us. **If** we confess our sins, he is faithful and just and will forgive us our sins and purify us from all unrighteousness (1 John 1:8–9).

Godprint: Repentance

Get Set

You'll need two small branches or craft sticks tied (or glued) together to form a cross, multicolored yarn, scissors. Optional: enough yarn and craft sticks for your group. Mark 1 John 1:8-9 in a Bible.

GO!

Today's Scripture verses are from the New Testament book of 1 John. Hand your Bible to a confident reader and ask him or her to read 1 John 1:8–9 aloud.

> **If we claim to be without sin, we deceive ourselves and the truth is not in us. If we confess our sins, he is faithful and just and will forgive us our sins and purify us from all unrighteousness.**

Flip back to Genesis 2:4 in your Bible and place it where your group can see it. **Let's take a trip back in time to the Old Testament and the story of Adam and Eve to better understand today's Scripture on sin and trickery. To visualize our passage I'll make a just-for-fun _time tunnel_ with my two sticks and yarn!**

Pick up the craft stick cross you brought with you and knot a long (24-inch length) of yarn at the center. As you tell the Adam and Eve story below, work the yarn from the center out and weave it under and over each stick until a small yarn "web" forms on the cross. For a different look, weave the yarn completely around each stick before moving on to next. Knot on longer strands of yarn if necessary to complete your fun time tunnel.

Adam and Eve lived a lovely life in a garden of fruit-ripened trees, crystal clear rivers, dew-moist pastures, and spicy perfumed flowers. Perhaps the days ended with a cloudless sky

with deepening shades of blue, peach, pink, and finally violet. Such beauty! Unfortunately, everything changes when Eve, the first woman on earth, chooses to take her lovely life into her own hands. While in the garden, Eve ponders the treacherous words of a voice other than her Creator, God. This "other voice," the serpent, is so persistent in his assurance that there is nothing to fear, Eve comes to believe him. *Eat from the forbidden tree*, the voice says.

- The serpent was a false teacher who did not bother to tell Adam and Eve that their disobedience would break their closeness with God. Have you had a friend tell you a tempting tale only to find out later you didn't get the whole story?
- Why is the "voice of wrong" so inviting to us? What can you do when God's quiet voice inside of you tells you to slow down before making a sinful choice?

Not only is the fruit pleasing to Eve's eye, but by eating it, she will gain the wisdom that only God possesses. Or so the serpent tells her. Eve eats the fruit and offers some to her mate, Adam. God discovers Adam and Eve's disobedience. Guilty and afraid, they listen as God outlines their painful future. But the story doesn't end there. God makes them "garments of skin" to wear. Adam and Eve will not leave the garden unprotected.

- What do we learn from the Adam and Eve story?

Yes! We can pretend that we are without sin. We can even convince others of the same. But we cannot deceive God who knows everything. When we repent and tell God we're sorry, he listens, disciplines fairly, and forgives the sin. Hold up the completed "time tunnel" and ask kids to imagine jumping inside to another time and place. **Wherever you find yourself, our faithful and just God is there.** If you wish, have enough supplies on hand for all in your group to make a time tunnel during your talk or for home use. Encourage children to share today's story and truth with their parents.

Be Well, Stay Warm

On Your Mark

Bible Truth: We show our faith in God when we show compassion to others.

Bible Verses: What good is it, my brothers, **if** a man claims to have faith but has no deeds? Can such faith save him? Suppose a brother or sister is without clothes and daily food. **If** one of you says to him, "Go, I wish you well; keep warm and well fed," but does nothing about his physical needs, what good is it? In the same way, faith by itself, if it is not accompanied by action, is dead (Jas. 2:14–17).

Godprint: Compassion

Get Set

You'll need an ample supply of items that you might give to a family in need, such as nonperishable food, jackets, and blankets. Make sure you have enough that it is obvious that you have plenty to share. Recruit a volunteer to help you by coming and asking for help. Mark James 2:14–17 in a Bible.

GO!

As kids gather, draw attention to your supplies. Pick up some food and say how delicious it is and that you can't wait until you can eat it. Spread out several jackets and say when you might wear each one. Keep this up until your volunteer comes in asking for help.

Follow this script or put the ideas in your own words:

Volunteer: Wow. I see you have a lot of food there. I haven't eaten in two days myself.

Pastor: Yes, I have some of my favorite foods here. I'm going to have a good dinner tonight.

Volunteer: I'm…I'm…really hungry.

Pastor: Well, I hope you find something to eat then. The restaurant just around the corner has some great lunch deals. (Turn to your jackets and rearrange them.)

Volunteer: I used to have a warm winter jacket. But it was stolen, and I don't have enough money to buy another one.

Pastor: If you just stay inside, I'm sure you'll keep warm. Winter will be over soon enough. (Smooth out the blankets.)

Volunteer: My apartment doesn't have any heat.

Pastor: Put an extra blanket on your bed. That should help. Thanks for stopping by. I wish you well.

Have your volunteer shuffle off looking disappointed, while you continue to admire your supplies.

Mmm. I wonder why he (she) was here. Do you have any ideas? Pause to let kids respond and let you know you should have done something to help!

I guess I missed a chance to show a little compassion, didn't I? Let's read some verses from the Bible. Ask a volunteer to read James 2:14–17.

> **What good is it, my brothers, if a man claims to have faith but has no deeds? Can such faith save him? Suppose a brother or sister is without clothes and daily food. If one of you says to him, "Go, I wish you well; keep warm and well fed," but does nothing about his physical needs, what good is it? In the same way, faith by itself, if it is not accompanied by action, is dead.**

- **According to these verses, what should I have done?**
- **What do you think it means that faith by itself is dead?** *(What we believe should show in what we do. God wants us to show our faith in him by our actions toward others.)*

God gave his Son, Jesus Christ, to die for us so that we can know God. When we know God, we want to be like him and do the things he would do. Our faith comes alive! God doesn't give us faith so that we can keep on living our lives just the way we always did. No, we're different. Faith pushes us into action. Faith gives us compassion toward people who need our help. That's living faith.

Bow for prayer. **Lord, thank you for helping us to know you. Help us also to do the things you want us to do. Open our eyes to people in need around us. Open our hearts so that we want to help. Open our pantries and closets so we can put feet on our faith. In Jesus' name, amen.**

You might want to use this children's sermon to kick off a food or clothing collection that your whole congregation can participate in.

FUN Flyer

On Your Mark

Bible Truth: God wants us to ask him for wisdom when things get tough.
Bible Verse: **If** any of you lacks wisdom, he should ask God, who gives generously to all without finding fault, and it will be given to him (Jas. 1:5).
Godprint: Wisdom

Get Set

You'll need a sheet of paper, copies of page 48, and a sample airplane that flies well. Mark James 1:5 in a Bible.

GO!

• **Who can make a great paper airplane?**
• **Can anyone share with us the science behind paper airplanes?**

Hand a sheet of paper to the youngest member in your group, with a request to make a paper airplane the best he or she can. Reassure your volunteer that it does not have to be perfect. Give the completed plane a whirl.

Great job, _____ (name of your volunteer). **But it's not easy, is it, making a paper plane that flies well? There's more to a paper airplane than a couple of folds. As we've seen, they have to be the right folds—or the plane will take a nosedive. True wisdom gives us the understanding to do things right and well. Our heavenly Father promises us that he will provide the wisdom we need to lead lives centered in him. And we don't need to feel foolish asking him for help.**

Open your Bible to James 1:5 and read the verse aloud to your group.

If any of you lacks wisdom, he should ask God, who gives generously to all without finding fault, and it will be given to him.

After reading the Scripture, pick up the tried and true airplane you brought with you and throw it. Watch as your children marvel at its staying power.

Distribute copies of the airplane on page 48 to all your children. **Now you get to make the** perfect paper flyer. Listen while you work as I share the wisdom behind the great paper airplane!

A well-folded plane works on a cushion of air. Even though we can't see it, this cushion of air is trapped under the wings. When thrown, the airplane floats along on this air cushion. Why? Because the air moves faster over the top of the wing than underneath. The faster-moving air has less pressure than the slower-moving air underneath. The greater pressure underneath pushes the plane upwards. This effect is called the "Bernoulli principle" after Daniel Bernoulli, a Swiss mathematician who lived in the mid-1700s.

There! Now you're as smart as I am! Have I impressed you with my wisdom? I hope not. This information can be found in any science book. But a truly great teacher gave the wisdom I now share with you about today's Scripture. Listen carefully as I pass it on to you. Respect the greatness of God and live according to his Word. Then ask for the wisdom you need. Don't be surprised when God answers!

Allow children a few minutes to give their airplanes a chance to soar. Give your volunteer the airplane you brought to class as a small thank you for his or her help today.

Before children leave, say, **Oh, by the way, my teacher's name? Jesus!**

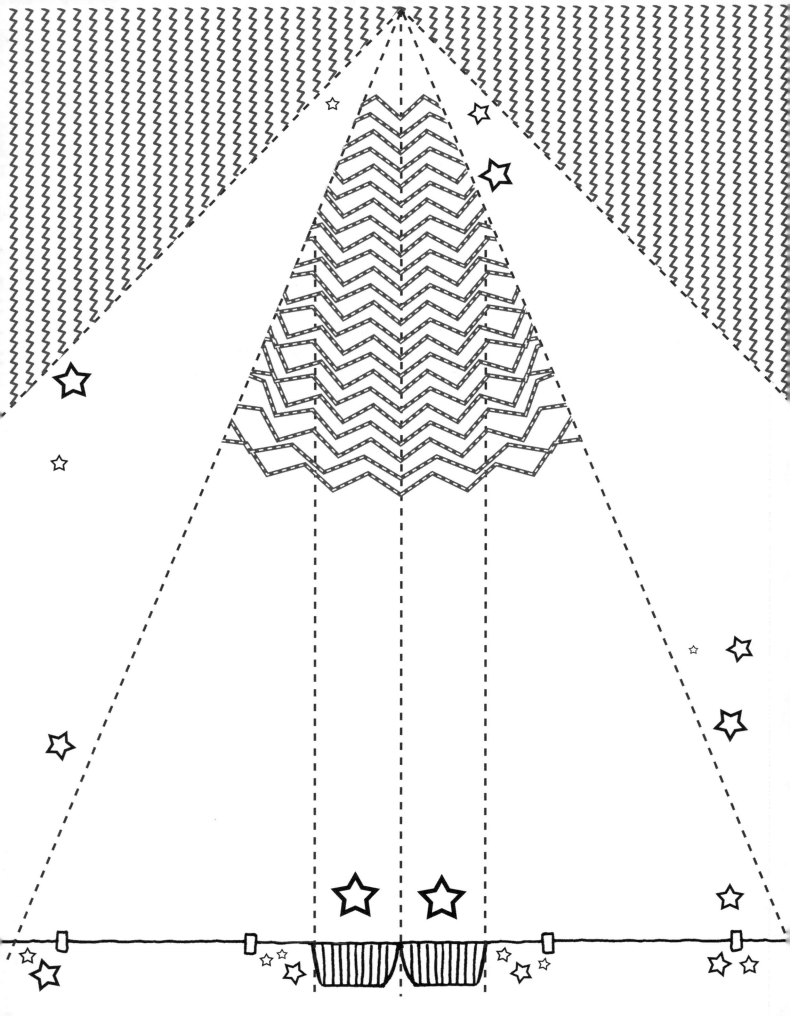

ANDS

A Sorry Sack

On Your Mark

Bible Truth: We can be thankful that we find rest in Jesus

Bible Verses: Come to me, all you who are weary **and** burdened, **and** I will give you rest. Take my yoke upon you **and** learn from me, for I am gentle **and** humble in heart, and you will find rest for your souls. For my yoke is easy **and** my burden is light (Matt. 11:28–30).

Godprint: Thankfulness

Get Set

You'll need music from a CD or tape and a CD or tape player, a large laundry bag filled with heavy winter clothing: woolen gloves or mittens, hats, earmuffs, snow boots, scarves, etc. **Or** heavy adult socks, sweaters, sweatshirts, and pants, work gloves, and hats. Mark Matthew 11:28–30 in a Bible.

GO!

Today's Scripture is a favorite for many, many people. It speaks of rest from work, school, and decisions that are hard to make. Open your Bible to Matthew 11:28–30 and read the verses aloud.

> **Come to me, all you who are weary and burdened, and I will give you rest. Take my yoke upon you and learn from me, for I am gentle and humble in heart, and you will find rest for your souls. My yoke is easy and my burden is light.**

- **A yoke is a heavy wooden harness fitted to the shoulders of oxen. This device allows an oxen team to pull a wagon or sled. Knowing that, what does this verse mean to you?**
- **Who gives us rest? (Jesus.) How is the yoke of Jesus different than, let's say, that of an oxen team pulling a wagon of heavy rocks?**

Homework. Chores. After-school sports. Taking care of the dog. Mom and Dad worries. These are burdens and troubles that weigh on children.

- **Like heavy books in a backpack, what burdens do children your age carry around?**
- **How does a restful nap or a good night's sleep help you face the tasks of a new day?**

Let's see if we can come up with a fun way to demonstrate the weight of kid "burdens."

Turn on the music from your CD or tape player. Hand the bag filled with clothes to a child nearest you. Tell the child (and your group) not to look inside the bag, but to simply pass the bag from one to another. When the music stops, whoever is left "holding the bag" is to open it, and without looking inside, pull out an item of clothing and put it on.

Continue to play the music and stop it now and again, allowing children to pull out items and put them on. Don't forget to reach into the bag and find a "burden" for you to wear!

Wearing mittens and boots inside may be fun, but they will eventually get in our way and slow us down. Not to mention how hot we'll get in just a little while. Time to shed your burdens! As you end your lesson, have children remove their items and drop them back into the bag.

Ahhh. That's better! We need to remember that burdens will always be a part of our lives. But Jesus doesn't want us to be overwhelmed by them. In God's kingdom his love and peace are what's important. When we put on the love and gentleness of Jesus, instead of the worries and burdens of the day, we're able to handle things calmly, ever thankful for his help.

Two in One

On Your Mark

Bible Truth: When we know Jesus, we know God.
Bible Verse: I **and** the Father are one (John 10:30).
Godprint: Wonder

Get Set

You'll need two different colors of play dough and a cutting board or some waxed paper. Depending on the size of your group, you may want to have several sets of play dough colors in action. Mark John 10:30 in a Bible.

GO!

I've got a challenge for you. I've got two different colors of play dough here. But I only want one color. So I want you to put these two colors of play dough together so they look like they were never separate. You might want to choose a couple of volunteers for this task, or give every child a little bit of each color. As they roll the two colors together, a third color will emerge. Encourage kids to keep rolling the dough until they are sure that the two colors look like they were always together. Collect a couple of samples of the play dough. Hold them up and look at them with a puzzled expression on your face.

Mmm. This doesn't look like the colors I gave you at all. Where are my two colors? Pause for responses. **Do you mean that I can't have two different colors, but have them look like they were never separate?** Pause for responses. **Blue and yellow make green. Red and blue make purple. Red and yellow make orange. Two colors can't make one color without changing.**

It's pretty hard for us to make two things into one thing without turning them into something else. But God can do something that we can't do. Jesus once was teaching a crowd of people when some of the religious leaders wanted to know if he thought he was God. They did not understand how Jesus could do the miracles he was doing. They thought that no one could be God. But let's find out how Jesus answered them. Ask a volunteer to read John 10:30.

I and my Father are one.

• What do you think Jesus meant by these six little words? *(He is not separate from God. He is the same as God.)*
• Why is the little word "and" important in this verse? *(Because it means that Jesus is the same as God.)*

Jesus wanted the people to know that he was doing miracles in the name of his Father. He could do that because he was one with his Father. That doesn't mean just that they were very close and got along really well. It doesn't mean just that Jesus listened to his Father and did what God said. It means that Jesus is God! "I and my Father are one." The people who saw Jesus doing miracles were seeing God. And when we know Jesus, we know God! Let's thank God for that.

Bow for prayer. **Dear Father, we're so amazed that you and Jesus are one. Sometimes that's hard for us to understand, even when we're grown-ups. But we thank you that when we know Jesus, we know God, because Father and Son are one. In Jesus' name, amen.**

Super Bowl

On Your Mark

Bible Truth: Jesus shows us the way to know God.

Bible Verse: I am the way and the truth and the life. No one comes to the Father except through me (John 14:6).

Godprint: Faith

Get Set

You'll need a popular consumer magazine, salt, sugar or sugar-substitute packets, baking soda, powdered sugar, four small dessert bowls, and a tray. Mark John 14:6 in a Bible.

GO!

As kids gather, open the magazine to a full-page ad for a low-fat food or food supplement. **TV commercials and magazine advertisements influence the things we do and say. Many claim that they can "show us the way" to live a long and happy life. If the spokesperson is convincing enough, we may even run out to buy the yummy dinner, cartoon character cereal, or triple fudge sundae!**

• Name a few things you simply can't live without. Why are they so important to you?

Place the tray and dessert bowls on your lap (or table.) **Here are a few super bowls—things I can't live without!** Sprinkle salt in a little pile in a dessert bowl. **Just a shake or two of salt helps bring out the flavor of my low-fat french fries!** Sprinkle sugar in dessert bowl #2. **And a low-calorie sweetener in my coffee every morning is a must.** Pour a small amount of baking soda in dessert bowl #3. **Baking soda has no fat or calories and gives my fresh-baked cake sponginess and height.** Finally, pour some powdered sugar into your last dessert bowl. **A sprinkle or two of powdered sugar will give me just the energy I need to run the two-minute mile!** Put the ingredient boxes aside and then switch the cups on the tray. Switch the cups again and again.

Oops! Now I'm all mixed up. I don't know which ingredient is which. They all look the same. Which one will I sprinkle on my french fries? Have kids try and guess the bowl that holds the salt.

Each cup on my tray holds appeal and promise of good things. But if I don't know which

one is which, how do I know what I'm getting? In other words, we don't know all the answers even when it looks right! But there is no guessing with today's Scripture. Jesus *is* the way to his Father. To know Jesus is to know the Father. Open your Bible and read John 14:6.

> I am the way and the truth and the life. No one comes to the Father except through me.

• We cannot see God in heaven. But at one time Jesus walked the earth and many people saw him. Still, it was very hard for Jews and Gentiles to believe that Jesus was the Son of God. What do you think would happen if Jesus came to live in your neighborhood? Would people today be more open to his teachings? Why or why not?

Simple. Sincere. Truthful. Only through Jesus can we connect with his Father in heaven. Accept no substitute! For a long and happy afterlife let's learn all we can about the Son of God, Jesus. Jesus is the way, the truth, and the path to eternal life.

Oops!

On Your Mark

Bible Truth: God wants us to make choices that please him so he can bless us.

Bible Verse: Do what is right **and** good in the LORD's sight, so that it may go well with you (Deut. 6:18).

Godprint: Obedience

Get Set

You'll need a square of cardboard about three feet by three feet, a dark permanent marker, masking tape, and beanbags. Mark Deuteronomy 6:18 in a Bible. Ahead of time, use the marker to divide the cardboard square into four quadrants. Write "Oops" on two of the squares, "Good" on one, and "Right" on the last section. Use the masking tape to mark off a line a few feet back from the square. (You can adjust this distance according to the age and ability of your kids.)

GO!

Choose two kids to help you with this presentation. If you would like more congregational involvement, recruit one adult and one child. Have the volunteers stand behind the masking tape line, facing the cardboard square.

We're going to play our own version of "foursquare" today. I have a cardboard foursquare right here and two beanbags.

- **Who can tell me what these words say?**
- **How do you think you can win this game?**

The way to win is to get one beanbag on the "good" space and one beanbag on the "right" space. You have to hit right _and_ good to win. One of our volunteers will be the tosser and the other will be the coach. If the tosser has trouble hitting both words, the coach will give some advice and the tosser will try again.

Take a minute or two to have the tosser throw the beanbags. (Make sure the distance is far enough to be challenging; move the cardboard if necessary.) If the first two beanbags don't land on the right squares, then it's the coach's turn to give advice to the tosser about how to aim or throw better. Depending on how many kids you have and how much time is available, you can decide whether to give more kids a turn to play. If a player hits both words, make sure to give a round of applause. After the game, collect the beanbags.

- **Can you win this game if you only land on one of the words?** (*No.*)
- **Why do you suppose I chose the words "right" and "good" for the winning words?**

Open your Bible to Deuteronomy 6:18. **In Deuteronomy 6:18 the Bible says, "Do what is right and good in the Lord's sight, so that it may go well with you."**

- **What do you think "so that it may go well with you" means?**
- **How do we obey God when we do what is right and good?**
- **How do we know what is right and good in the Lord's eyes?** (*The Bible tells us. Pastors, parents, and teachers help us learn.*)

When we do what is right and good, we obey God. And when we obey God, we please him. God wants to bless us when we please him. We all make an "oops" once in a while. Sometimes we try to do the right thing, but we miss. Maybe we get mad at a little brother, or we talk back to a parent, or we don't want to share something we really like to play with. But God always gives us another chance. We can try again to do what is right and good, just like our tosser got to try again to hit the right squares. Remember, right *and* good.

Bow for prayer. **Father, we thank you that when we make an oops, you give us another chance to do what is right and good. And we thank you that when we do what is right and good in your eyes, you bless us. Help us to take the best aim we can to do what is right and good. Amen.**

Face It!

On Your Mark

Bible Truth: God wants us to live in the grace and peace that he gives us.
Bible Verse: Grace **and** peace to you from God our Father **and** the Lord Jesus Christ (Phil. 1:2).
Godprint: Joy of discipleship

Get Set

You'll need some mirrors. Optional: paper plates and a variety of facial features cut from pictures in magazines, craft and glue sticks. Mark Philippians 1:2 in a Bible.

GO!

Today's Scripture verse comes from the book of Philippians. This Bible book is a heart-felt letter written by the Apostle Paul to the people in the town of Philippi. Paul could not talk to them in person because he was in a desperate place—he was in prison. Yet joy is what we hear when we read today's verse.

Read Philippians 1:2 from your Bible or ask a volunteer to read.

Grace and peace to you from God our Father and the Lord Jesus Christ.

Wherever Paul found himself, in believer's homes, resting under an olive tree, chained and in prison, his relationship with Jesus is the thing that keeps him going. Hungry or well fed, tired or well rested, in pain or feeling fine, Paul claimed his joy. His strength and mission to spread the Word came from his connection to the risen Jesus. We can learn to follow Paul's example when we feel down or unhappy.

• How many feelings can we name? *(Happy, sad, angry, loving, annoyed, hurt, uneasy, calm, unsure, joyful, surprised, bored, compassionate, humble, peaceful, kind, self-controlled, faithful.)*
• How many of these feelings do you think you experience throughout the day?

Let's "make faces" to match the feelings of an average day.

Distribute mirrors or the paper plates. Ask your children to make faces in the mirror or form faces on paper plates with the features cut from magazines you brought with you.

Make a face (in the mirror or on the plate) **that matches the first feeling we mentioned, *happy*.** Once children perform the action, have them repeat today's Scripture verse with their "happy faces" in place.

Grace and peace to you from God our Father and the Lord Jesus Christ. Philippians 1:2

That wasn't so hard, was it? Good! Let's make a face to match the feeling of *anger*. Pause. **Now with your angry face on repeat today's verse after me.**

- **Raise your hand if you found it difficult "to be angry" and repeat today's verse of grace and peace.**
- **How do you think a visitor to our church might feel if you were speaking to him or her?** *(Confused, a bit frightened.)*

Continue "making faces" (sad, disappointed, lost, surprised) as time permits.

Others know we are Christians by the joy and gentleness we wear. Our example will make them comfortable and invite them to discover the reason for the peace we feel. Happily we can tell them of the wonderfulness of our Savior and King, Jesus Christ.

Option: If you wish, have children glue the expression that made them feel the most joyful onto the paper plate. The upper portion of a craft stick glued to the back of the paper plate makes for a good handle.

I'm chewing on the morsel of a proverb;
    I'll let you in on the sweet old truths,
Stories we heard from our fathers,
    counsel we learned at our mother's knee.
We're not keeping this to ourselves,
    we're passing it along to the next
    generation—
GOD's fame and fortune,
    the marvelous things he has done.
He planted a witness in Jacob,
    set his Word firmly in Israel,
Then commanded our parents
    to teach it to their children
So the next generation would know,
    and all the generations to come—
Know the truth and tell the stories
    so their children can trust in God,
Never forget the works of God
    but keep his commands to the letter.

Psalm 78:2–7 *The Message*

For an answer Jesus called over a child, whom he stood in the middle of the room, and said, "I'm telling you, once and for all, that unless you return to square one and start over like children, you're not even going to get a look at the kingdom."

Matthew 18:2–3 *The Message*

He put a child in the middle of the room. Then, cradling the little one in his arms, he said, "Whoever embraces one of these children as I do embraces me, and far more than me—God who sent me."

Mark 9:36-37 *The Message*

What marvelous love the Father has extended to us! Just look at it—we're called children of God! That's who we really are.

1 John 3:1 *The Message*

Yeah, God!

Bible Truth: We can ask God for help in hard times because he is good.
Bible Verse: You are forgiving **and** good, O Lord, abounding in love to all who call to you (Ps. 86:5).
Godprint: Forgiveness

Get Set

Ahead of time, write the following words on index cards: kind, loving, gracious, faithful, holy, great, mighty, merciful. Mark Psalm 86:5 in a Bible.

GO!

As kids gather, moan and groan a little about the hard week you've had. **I'm so glad it's the weekend, because I sure need a break. I worked so hard this week that my bones are complaining. I don't mind working hard for something I want, but this week it seemed like everything went wrong. I didn't get my work done, somebody made fun of me and hurt my feelings, I got in trouble for something I didn't even do—you get the picture. It was a tough week!**

Sometimes I feel like I'm the only person in the world who has it tough. But then I read in the Bible about a guy like David. Now he had it tough! God had chosen him to be king, but he had to wait 40 years till he could have the job. In the meantime he had to live in caves and be on the run. His enemies didn't just make fun of him, they wanted to kill him. That's a pretty tough life.

David had times when he wondered if it was all worth it. He moaned and groaned and asked God to take revenge on his enemies. But even in the middle of complaining, David remembered some important things about God. Let's find out what. Ask a volunteer to read Psalm 86:5.

You are forgiving and good, O Lord, abounding in love to all who call to you.

• **How does David describe God in this verse?**
• **Why do you think David chose these words to use in the middle of a tough time?**
• **What does "all who call to you" mean?**

David said God was forgiving *and* good. He knew that it was out of God's kindness that God answers prayers, even when we need forgiveness. No matter how much we moan and groan, God is still good.

I've got some words here to help us remember what God is like in tough times. Pass out the index cards to some of the kids. Make sure they are independent readers.

I'll say the words "Lord, you are" and then point to someone with a card. If I point to you, you fill in the blank with the word on your card. Then the rest of us all say together, "Yea, God!" Ready? Lord, you are … point to a child. Continue until you have used all the cards. Be sure to encourage the congregation to join in on "Yea, God!"

Good job! Now let's make it a little harder. This time we'll do it without cards and think of our own words. I'm going to point to one person, who quickly says a word. Then I'll say "and" and point to someone else. After the second word, we'll all say, "Yea, God!" Ready? Lord, you are _____ (point to one child) **and _____** (point to a second child). If you have mostly younger children, you may want to let them know that it is all right to repeat one of the words already used.

God is forgiving and good—and loving, and mighty, and faithful, and_____. Mention some of the words that kids have given. **Like David, we know that no matter how tough the times get, we can call on him and he will hear us. Let's thank him for that right now.**

Bow for prayer. **Lord, you are forgiving and good. Thank you that no matter what mistakes we make, you forgive us. Thank you that your love for us is overflowing. Thank you for hearing us when we call on you. Amen.**

Stylish Threads

On Your Mark

Bible Truth: God wants us to show that we know him in the way we treat others.
Bible Verse: As God's chosen people ... clothe yourselves with compassion, kindness, humility, gentleness **and** patience (Col. 3:12).
Godprint: Kindness

Get Set

You'll need used dryer softener sheets, some baby pictures, a jacket, sweatshirt, or sweater for a volunteer in your group, pens. Mark Colossians 3:12 in a Bible.

GO!

I have some babies today I'd like you to meet! Hold up or pass around the baby pictures you brought with you. **Babies may not say a lot we understand, but ask any parent and he or she will tell you that babies are brilliant!**

• **What have Mom or Dad told you about your baby times?**
• **What were your first words?**

Babies treated with kindness know they are loved. Babies yearn to be comforted and touched in loving, gentle ways.

We, too, want to be treated gently and know that we are loved. Open your Bible to Colossians 3:12. Offer your seat and Bible to a confident reader to read the Scripture to the group.

> **As God's chosen people ... clothe yourselves with compassion, kindness, humility, gentleness and patience.**

"As God's chosen people" we are to live like Christ, clothed or "displayed" in his gentle ways, demonstrating his loving behavior. Ask your volunteer to put on the jacket or sweater you brought and model it for the group. **You look mighty stylish, Christopher** (substitute the name of your volunteer), **but I think we can do better than that!**

Look to your group. **Now the rest of you get to help. Think of ways children can show compassion or tenderness to others.** Point to the dryer sheets. **Once you do, pick up a dryer sheet from my pile and write a few words or draw a simple picture on the sheet. After sharing your idea with the group, walk over and "clothe" our wonderful volunteer in dryer sheet compassion!**

Have three or four volunteers respond and then come up and stick their dryer sheets on your volunteer's jacket.

Now, let's name some ways children can show kindness. Continue this activity with each of the Christ attributes mentioned in today's verse (humility, gentleness and patience). By the time your group finishes, your volunteer should be stylishly clothed in godly characteristics.

As difficult as it is to be gentle and humble and patient, Christ's Spirit works within us to be more like him.

Option: If you wish, use small, inflated balloons in place of the dryer sheets. After each response, ask children to rub their balloons against their hair, creating static electricity, and stick them to the volunteer's jacket.

I Hear That Voice

On Your Mark

Bible Truth: Because God is our Savior, we have hope.
Bible Verse: Guide me in your truth **and** teach me, for you are God my Savior, **and** my hope is in you all day long (Ps. 25:5).
Godprint: Hope

Get Set

You'll need a blindfold, and a marker and sheet of paper. Make a large dot in one corner of the paper. Mark Psalm 25:5 in a Bible.

GO!

Do we have any budding young artists in the crowd today? Anyone who would like to draw us a picture? Choose a volunteer and have him or her move close to you. Hand the volunteer the marker.

Oh, I left out a couple of details. You're going to wear this blindfold while you draw. Pause to put the blindfold securely on the volunteer.

Now I need a couple more volunteers. I promise you won't have to wear a blindfold. Recruit two more helpers.

Say to the artist volunteer, **I hope you're a good listener, because you're going to need your ears. I have a sheet of paper with a dot on it. Your job is to get from the other edge of the paper to the dot with the marker. One of these two volunteers** (point to the first volunteer) **is going to help you by telling where you need to go on the paper. But the other one** (point to the second volunteer) **is going to give you some bad advice. You have to try to figure out who to listen to. We'll see how far you get in 30 seconds. Ready? Go!** Make sure the paper is directly in front of the blindfolded volunteer. After 30 seconds, call time. Remove the blindfold and see how the artist did. Ask the artist:

• **How did you feel about what I asked you to do?**
• **How did you figure out who you should listen to?**
Listening to the right guidance makes a big difference in how we feel and the choices we

make. **Let's look at a Bible verse about that**. Ask a volunteer to read Psalm 25:5.

> **Guide me in your truth and teach me, for you are God my Savior, and my hope is in you all day long.**

• **What is the psalmist asking God to do?** *(Guide and teach.)*
• **Why should we ask God to guide us?** *(He is our Savior.)*
• **What do you think it means to hope in God all day long?**

We see the word "and" two times in this verse. The psalmist asks God to guide and teach him. The reason is because God is Savior and we can hope in him. When we ask God to guide us and teach us, we can be sure that he'll show us how to go the right way. We don't have to figure things out all by ourselves, as if we have a blindfold on. God's voice is the one to listen to. That fills us with hope—all day, every day.

Bow for prayer. **God, you are our Savior. Thank you that you guide us and teach us in the true way to go. We're so glad that we can hope in you. In your name, amen.**

Bear with Me!

On Your Mark

Bible Truth: God wants us to forgive when we are hurt by others.

Bible Verse: Bear with each other **and** forgive whatever grievances you may have against one another (Col. 3:13).

Godprint: Forgiveness

Get Set

You'll need a plush bear. Optional: a steaming mug of coffee, tea, or your favorite beverage, reading glasses. Mark Colossians 3:13 in a Bible.

GO!

Open your Bible to Colossians 3:13 and hand it to a confident reader. Grab hold of the plush teddy bear you brought with you and give it a hug! **Bear on board! I'd like you to meet Mr. Bearable. I like taking him along when I talk to children about today's Bible verse, Colossians 3:13.** Ask your reader to read the verse aloud from your Bible.

> **Bear with each other and forgive whatever grievances you may have against one another.**

Mr. Bearable is a great reminder of what the Apostle Paul instructs us to do in today's Scripture. He wants us to **bear** with one another when friends act up and annoy us or even when they lie, cheat, or hurt us. And not only that…we're not to turn into bears—all growls and angry snarls when someone does us wrong.

Even when the hurtful actions of others cause us to get so angry we can't see straight—God wants us to forgive them. Ask each in your group to hold up their pointer finger an arm's length away from their faces. With eyes on their fingers, ask them to bring them slowly toward their noses. One straight finger should soon turn into two blurry ones!

Those fingers were straight a minute ago, weren't they? That's how quickly our feelings can turn from tender and loving to angry and spiteful. Yet, even in those times when it's most difficult, Christ asks us to imitate him and bear with one another in love.

Hold up Mr. Bearable again. ***Growl. Growl.*** **I know that this Scripture verse is hard to put into action. It's hard for big people as well.**

- **On a scale of 1 to 10, how hard is it for you to forgive someone who knocks over your bike on purpose or makes fun of you in the school cafeteria?**
- **If it's that hard, how does God expect us to forgive those who wrong us?** *(We must rely on Christ's power to ease our anger and make a way for forgiveness.)*

Only with Christ's help can we be forgiving and allow love to guide our lives. And, remember, Christ is not asking us to do anything he hasn't done himself. His love for us was so strong that he took our sins, the ones we commit over and over again, to the cross and died that they might not be held against us. Praise him for his love and steadfastness.

Optional: Here's another way to demonstrate how anger keeps us from seeing in love. Put on a pair of reading glasses and take a sip from a steaming mug of coffee or tea. After taking a sip—blow. The hot beverage will cause steam to form on your glasses and temporarily blur your vision. You may need to take a couple of sips so everyone sees your "I'm so mad I can't see straight!" expression.

On the Grow

Bible Truth: We're never too old to know Jesus better.
Bible Verse: Grow in the grace **and** knowledge of our Lord **and** Savior Jesus Christ (2 Pet. 3:18).
Godprint: Discipleship

Get Set

You'll need a brown paper grocery sack, tape, markers, and enough copies of page 72 that every child can have a leaf. If possible, make the copies on green paper. Cut out the leaves ahead of time. Slit the bag open on the sides so it is one long strip. Mark 2 Peter 3:18 in a Bible.

GO!

It looks like we have people of all sizes here, small and tall, we love 'em all. Let's find out who is the smallest and the tallest. Have kids line up according to height. You may want to ask another adult from the congregation to help you arrange the kids. If you want to extend the line, have middle school kids join, or even adults.

It looks like _____ (name) is the smallest and _____ (name) is the tallest. Why do you think that is? *(Most likely the smallest is also one of the youngest, and the tallest is one of the oldest.)* **It looks like some of us have been growing longer than others.** Have everyone sit down.

• **Do we ever stop growing?** *(Yes, we reach an adult height and do not get any taller than that.)*
• **Name some other things that grow.** *(Animals, plants, trees.)*
• **What would it be like if we never stopped growing?** *(Pause for kids to speculate.)*

Let's read a verse from the Bible about growing. Ask a volunteer to read 2 Peter 3:18.

Grow in the grace and knowledge of our Lord and Savior Jesus Christ.

• **What do you think it means to grow in the grace of our Lord and Savior?** *(To be more like Jesus, to live the way God wants us to live.)*

- **What does it mean to grow in knowledge?** *(To know more about God, to understand the Bible better, to know what right teaching is.)*
- **Why does this verse tell us to grow in grace and knowledge?** *(God wants us to know the truth about him, but he also wants us to become like him.)*
- **Can we ever know too much about being like Jesus?**

A tree is something that grows for a very long time, sometimes hundreds of years. We're going to make a tree of grace and knowledge to remind us that God wants us to keep on growing.

Pass out the leaf cutouts and markers. If you have mostly younger children or a large group, you may prefer to do the writing yourself. **On this leaf, you can write or draw a way that you can keep on growing to be more like Jesus. Then we'll tape all our leaves to this trunk** (grocery sack) **for a tree of grace and knowledge.** If your time is limited, you may want to ask a teen or adult to help with this process as well. Or have the kids tape leaves on the trunk without writing on them.

That's a great tree. Whenever we look at it, we'll remember to keep on growing in the grace and knowledge of Jesus. If possible, hang the tree of grace in a place where the children and others will see it for a few weeks.

Close in prayer. **Lord, we thank you that you made our bodies to grow. And we thank you that our spirits grow as well. Help us to know you better and better and never get tired of growing in grace. In your name, amen.**

Leaf Patterns

BUTS

Memory Makers

On Your Mark

Bible Truth: God wants us to rest so we can serve him better.
Bible Verses: Six days you shall labor and do all your work, **but** the seventh day is a Sabbath to the LORD your God (Exod. 20:9–10).
Godprint: Reverence

Get Set

You'll need a visor or sun hat; suntan lotion; beach blankets; the word "rest" printed on poster board surrounded by cloud and/or star stickers; the word "worship" printed on poster board with a picture of your church; the word "relief" printed on poster board surrounded by leaf stickers. Mark Exodus 20:9-10 in a Bible.

GO!

Spread the beach blankets out and have your children sit. Splash on some suntan lotion!

Sometimes the best part of summer vacation is not the sun, surf, or sand—but the time after. By that I mean when the snow or chilly rains come, it's great fun to relive our memories of the warm and fun days of summer.

- **What was your best summer vacation? What made it fun to remember lately?**
- **Raise your hand if your family has photo albums, memory books, or videos of your last summer vacation. When would be a good time to look at them again?**

Today's Old Testament Scripture is from the Book of Exodus.

Open your Bible to Exodus 20:9–10 and read the verses aloud.

> Six days you shall labor and do all your work, but the seventh day is a Sabbath to the LORD your God.

Hold high the "rest" poster board for the group to see. **In his great wisdom, God commands us to spend time in rest each week. It's a necessity! School days and workdays are filled with** busyness and things to do. All in all, these things distract, lead us away, from our center, our faith in God our Father. Setting aside time to rest gives us the chance to let the busy week go. We can spend time with our Creator and think back upon his blessings. Like a lazy-hazy day on the beach, it refreshes our "insides"—our connection to God—and puts a smile on our faces!

• How do you feel the next day when you haven't had a good night's rest? On a scale from 1 to 10, how hard is it to get through the day?

Sleep, too, is a requirement of our bodies. We can try to stay awake, commanding our eyes to stay open, but eventually our eyes will close. We cannot ignore our bodies' need for sleep.

Hold up the "worship" poster board. **In the same way, we must not ignore our need for worship. Our faith and connection to our Creator depends on it. Scripture tells us that God never sleeps** (Ps. 121:3-4). **He's watchful and on call every minute of the day. We are not alone. In worship, we rejoice and sing praises to God, thanking him for his angels, who surround and protect us. How sad if we let the things of the world keep us from worshiping and hearing Scripture's words of rest and comfort.**

Finally, hold up the poster board with the word "relief" printed. Have an older child read the word.

Is *relief* (emphasize as re-***leaf***) **only something trees do in the spring? Of course not! But think of it as a word to remember today's wise and restful Scripture. We find relief, rest, and comfort in worship.**

Many to One

On Your Mark

Bible Truth: God gives us strength when we do something hard.
Bible Verse: "**But** Lord," Gideon asked, "how can I save Israel? My clan is the weakest in Manasseh, and I am the least in my family" (Judg. 6:15).
Godprint: Confidence

Get Set

You'll need a rope long enough to play tug-o-war. Mark Judges 6:15 in a Bible.

GO!

As kids gather around you, flex your arm muscles. **I've been working out a lot lately, trying to build up my muscles. What do you think? Am I getting stronger?** Invite two or three kids to feel your arm muscle. **I have a feeling I'd better keep working out. You never know when you're going to need strength to do something hard.**

Take out the rope and start unrolling it. **In fact, I've got something right here that might be hard. Let's see, I need one person to hang on to the end of this rope.** Regardless of who volunteers, select the youngest or smallest child in your group.

(Name of child) **is going to hang on to one end of this rope. Guess what the rest of you are going to do.** Pause for responses. **You're all going to hang on to the other end of the rope. Then when I say "Go," everybody will pull.** Allow some time for all the kids to grab hold of the rope. (If you have a large group, you can do this activity with a few volunteers, as long as you have one small child against several bigger, stronger kids.)

• **What do you think is going to happen?** *(The larger team will win.)*
• **How would you feel if you had to play against so many people?**

Let's see what happens. Stand near the small child. **Ready? Go!** As the larger groups pulls, make sure the small child is safe. Afterward, collect the rope and have the kids sit down.

(Name of child) **never really had a chance. You all thought the big group would win, and it** did. The Bible has a story where the little team won. It's a story about Gideon. The Israelites were having a tough time. The Midianites, their enemies, kept stealing or destroying all their food and animals. The Israelites didn't know what to do. That's when God came to Gideon and told him that Gideon would be the one to win over the Midianites. Let's find out what Gideon had to say about that.

Ask a volunteer to read Judges 6:15.

> "But Lord," Gideon asked, "how can I save Israel? My clan is the weakest in Manasseh, and I am the least in my family."

• Why did Gideon say, "But Lord"? *(He didn't think it was possible. He wasn't an important person.)*
• How was Gideon feeling?

Who can tell us what happened in the story about Gideon? *(Gideon gathered an army of 30,000 men. The Lord told most of the army to go home. Gideon had only 300 men when he faced the Midianites. They smashed jars and blew trumpets and made so much noise that they scared off the Midianites without a battle.*
See Judges 6–7.)

When God told Gideon that he would be the one to save Israel, Gideon didn't think it was possible. He wasn't an important, famous person. His family weren't the leaders of Israel. And Gideon was the least important person in his family. So how could he save all the people? He said, "But Lord" the way you might say, "But (name of child) can't pull on that rope," or "But Mom, I can't do this by myself." But Gideon learned that when God wants us to do something, even when it's hard, there are no buts about it. He gives us the strength.

Bow for prayer. **Lord, thank you for being with us when we do hard things. Help us not to say, "But Lord." Instead, help us say, "Yes, Lord." We depend on your strength. Amen.**

What's in a Name?

On Your Mark

Bible Truth: We can always depend on God.

Bible Verse: Some trust in chariots and some in horses, **but** we trust in the name of the LORD our God (Ps. 20:7).

Godprint: Trust

Get Set

Mark Psalm 20:7 in a Bible.

GO!

As children gather, make a point to call as many by name as you can. **Come on over here _____. I'm glad to see you, _____. There's a space for you right here, _____.**

Mmm. I know your first names and your last names, but I'm not so sure about your middle names. Can anyone tell me your middle name? Pause for responses. Put some whole names together, for example, "Robyn Leanne Richards," "Tyler James Prince."

You've got some pretty snazzy names. I'm sure your parents thought a long time about what to call you and came up with the name that's just perfect for you. If I say your name, everyone knows I'm talking about you!

Let's try out some other names. Some of these might be names that your parents remember, and some might be names that only kids think about. Whether you're a grown-up or a child, raise your hand if you know who I'm talking about when I say these names. Mention a variety of names that span generational knowledge, such as Captain Kangaroo and Mr. Green Jeans, Red Skelton, Bill Cosby, Mr. Rogers, Elmo, Barney, SpongeBob SquarePants. Use names from television, movies, or popular culture that you're pretty sure most people will recognize.

Let's think about names for someone who cares about us very much—God. The Bible uses many different names to help us understand more about God. How many names for God in the Bible can we think of? Invite the entire congregation to participate in calling out names of God. Here are a few to suggest if response is slow: the Almighty, Wonderful Counselor, Prince of

Peace, Abba Father, Lord, Creator, Good Shepherd, Savior, the Lamb, King of kings, Father of lights.

Let's read a verse about the name of the Lord. Ask a volunteer to read Psalm 20:7.

> **Some trust in chariots and some in horses, but we trust in the name of the Lord our God.**

- **Why do you think some people trust in chariots and horses?** *(Because they are strong, fast, powerful.)*
- **Why is it better to trust in the name of God?**

When we trust in the name of the Lord our God, we're not just talking about a word. All the different names for God in the Bible help us to know all the different ways that God loves and cares for us. He's a loving Shepherd, a merciful Savior, the one who gives us everything we need, the shield that protects us.

Some people might like to trust in things they can see, things that they know are strong—like chariots and horses in Bible times. But God wants us to trust in him. When we trust in the name of God, we trust God to be all the things that all his names say he is. There's nothing better.

Bow for prayer. **Lord God, Almighty God, our Father and our Savior, we thank you for your strong name and all the things you promise when we trust in your name. Remind us that we have you on our side. In Jesus' name, amen.**

Lite Brite

On Your Mark

Bible Truth: God want us to feel on the inside what we say on the outside.

Bible Verse: Anyone who claims to be in the light **but** hates his brother is still in the darkness (1 John 2:9).

Godprint: Honesty

Get Set

You'll need a white votive candle, desk and chair, glass of water, matches or lighter. Mark 1 John 2:9 in a Bible.

GO!

Hold the candle up for your children to see. **I have some truths to share about my little candle today. If you agree clap your hands.**

Fun Fact #1—My candle is white. Pause as children clap.

Fun Fact #2—My candle will burn bright once I light it. Pause as children clap.

Fun Fact #3—My candle is worth $1,000,000 dollars. Not much clapping!

Smart bunch! Unless there is a rare diamond buried deep in this candle, it is only worth a little bit of money. My two candle truths and one candle fib demonstrate that a lie bends the truth. When we don't tell the truth or when we're not honest with our friends or family, it's the lie that people remember most—and it weakens our connection to them.

• Do you agree with this statement: 99 percent of the truth is still a lie? Why or why not?

• How does dishonesty keep people in the dark?

God wants us to feel on the inside what we show the world on the outside. When we lie or mistreat or "get even" with others, we pretend to be "light and bright," but we live with a dishonest heart. Jesus, God's Son and the smartest man whoever lived, instructs us to live differently. And today's Scripture verse tells us so.

Open your Bible and read 1 John 2:9.

Anyone who claims to be in the light but hates his brother is still in the darkness.

These behaviors often hurt people in ways we do not intend. Dishonesty can have a long reach.

Light a votive candle and place it on the desk. Place the water-filled glass in front of the candle. **Let's say that the light behind the glass is a person having a fabulous day. But their joy is short-lived when a lie comes to call.** Ask a volunteer to sit on the chair and blow straight at the water glass. Amazingly, the lit candle **behind** the glass blows out.

You may say that you never intended for your best friend to get hurt, but your actions have taken on a life of their own. Falsehoods and hatred are not the actions of Christ. He wants us to be "light bright" both inside and out. With his help we can dissolve anger and hate and live in him.

Go in peace to serve the Lord of light and love.

No Bunny Loves You
the Way God Loves You!

Bible Truth: God deserves our glory and praise.
Bible Verse: Not to us, O LORD, not to us **but** to your name be the glory, because of your love and faithfulness (Ps. 115:1).
Godprint: Praise

Get Set

You'll need colorful index cards, paper clips and markers. *(Beware: paper clips are choking hazards for young children. If you have many preschoolers in your group, you may prefer to skip this activity or tape the paper clips securely to the index cards.)* Before the day of your talk, write on each of the index cards, **NO BUNNY LOVES YOU THE WAY GOD LOVES YOU!** On the day of your sermon, set the index cards in a pile, print side down, and place the paper clips and markers in separate bowls where kids can reach easily. Mark Psalm 115:1 in a Bible.

GO!

· Raise your hand if you've seen actors perform on a brightly lit stage.

So have I! Now I'd like you all to close you eyes for a moment and imagine something with me. Pause. **Picture yourself standing all alone on a dark, dark stage. It's so dark you can't see your hand in front of your face. You're not sure where the stage begins or ends and you don't want to fall off—so you stand perfectly still.**

Suddenly, a spotlight snaps on. It shines brightly on a spot about five feet from where you're standing. Ask children to open their eyes. **Tell me what might your reaction be upon seeing the light? What's the thing you'd most like to do?** *(Run into the spotlight; put on a show.)*

A sudden light in a dark place is a wonderful thing, isn't it? In the light we feel comforted and no longer alone. We're also very grateful that someone knows where we are and has come to our rescue. In today's Scripture that someone is God our Father. God speaks to us in today's Scripture verse from the Book of Psalms. Read the verse aloud from your Bible.
   Not to us, O LORD, not to us but to your name be the glory, because of your love

and faithfulness.

God deserves the spotlight, the glory, because of his great love and faithfulness for us. When we're lost and in the dark, he knows where we are. When we're afraid and alone, he won't leave us. Ever. We can always trust the love—as comforting as a warm bright light—of our Creator. God deserves the glory and praise for being our protector and provider.

And let's be sure to share the light with others. Everyone wants to be in the light. In other words…don't hog the spotlight! In fact, rather than (***snort, snort!***) be hogs, I prefer we be bunnies! Pass out the colorful index cards and have kids read the print aloud with you. ***"NO BUNNY LOVES YOU THE WAY GOD LOVES YOU!"*** Show your children how to slip two paper clips onto their cards (see diagram) to make long bunny ears. Pick up a marker and then drawer bunny eyes and bunny whiskers as the diagram suggests.

Slip your card it into your backpack or use it as a fun bookmark. Whatever you choose, keep it close. May it serve as a reminder that bunnies rule and hogs drool! God deserves the glory and praise because of his everlasting love and faithfulness.

Option: If you prefer to keep your group's cards for later use, store them using this simple technique: stretch 10 or 12 large rubber bands around a sturdy binder. Interlace the cards among the rubber bands.

Dee-Lightful!

On Your Mark

Bible Truth: God wants us to tell the truth.
Bible Verse: The LORD detests lying lips, **but** he delights in men who are truthful (Prov. 12:22).
Godprint: Honesty

Get Set

You'll need index cards and a marker. Put a bookmark at Proverbs 12:22 in a Bible. Ahead of time, write the following words on index cards, using a large capital "D" each time: Dog, Day, Date, Dance, Dark, Dare, Deer, Dig, Dip, Duck, Dust, Down. If any of the kids have names that begin with D, you may also want to use those.

GO!

As kids gather, shuffle your index cards. Say, **A, B, C, E, F, G. That doesn't sound right. Let me try again. A, B, C, E, F, G. That's still not right. What did I miss?** *(D!)* **Silly me, how could I miss D when I have a handful of words that begin with the letter D? Maybe you can help me read all the D words. I'll hold one up, and you call out what it says.**

Hold up the cards one at a time and let kids read the words to you. Say, "D is for _____" and have kids fill in the blank. Depending on the reading ability of your kids and the size of the group, you may want to be sure that everyone who wants to read a word has an opportunity to do so.

Okay, A, B, C, D, E, F, G. Now I've got it. I hope I won't ever forget D again. Thinking about the letter D makes me think of a Bible verse with some words that begin with the letter D. Let's read it. Ask a volunteer to read Proverbs 12:22.

> **The LORD detests lying lips, but he delights in men who are truthful.**

- **What two D words did you hear in this verse?** *(Detests, delights.)*
- **Can anyone tell us what those words mean?** *(Detest means to dislike or hate something. Delight means to take pleasure in something.)*
- **What does this verse say the Lord detests?** *(Lying.)* **What does the Lord delight in?** *(People who are truthful.)*

Detest and delight—those are a couple of hard D words, but they get right to the point. That little tiny word in between makes all the difference—"but." God tells us very clearly that he hates lying, but he loves it when we tell the truth.

Sometimes it seems a lot easier to tell a lie than to tell the truth. Maybe we think that a lie will help us get what we want or keep us out of trouble. We think it's not hurting anyone. But we're not fooling God. Let's show the Lord lots of reasons to be delighted with our truthfulness.

Bow for prayer. **Lord, every day we're tempted to tell lies, some big ones, some little ones. They're all wrong, and we're sorry. Help us to please you every day with lips that tell the truth. In Jesus' name, amen.**

Frequent Flyer Smiles

On Your Mark

Bible Truth: Be a cheerful friend and help others.
Bible Verse: An anxious heart weighs a man down, **but** a kind word cheers him up (Prov. 12:25).
Godprint: Friendliness

Get Set

You'll need an apron, jacket, or vest with pockets. Place a lemon, a tennis ball (or other small ball), and a watch in the pockets.

GO!

Smooth out your apron or jacket. **How do I look?** Pause for children to respond. **That's spiffy, huh? Thank you! My apron is colorful, but it's pretty loaded down today. Sadly, each pocket has something that children worry about.**

• **What would you say are the Top 3 Kid Worries?**
• **Is there something that others do for you that makes you feel better? What about cookies and milk? A hug? A smile?** Share your thoughts with the group.

Ask a volunteer to come up and reach into one of your pockets and pull out the contents.

Hold up the lemon. **Did you ever have this worry? You start the day lemony-bright but end up a sourpuss because you think the children at school don't like you?**

• **Is there someone who can help you when you feel sad or mad or anxious about school? Who?**

Throw the lemon in the air and catch it. **Good thinking! Worry buster #1: Your teacher, mom or dad, or friends are great people to tell you that you're a pretty good kid. Because you are! When they do, suddenly you feel a little better, don't you? A kind word or action is the ticket to keeping worries in check. This is the message in today's Scripture verse.** Open your Bible and read Proverbs 12:25. Ask your children to repeat it after you.

An anxious heart weighs a man down, but a kind word cheers him up.

Ask a second volunteer to dig into another pocket. **This ball can represent the many sports that children love to play at recess or after school. Making mistakes during practice or a game is a big worry for many kids. You go to kick the soccer ball—and miss! Or swing the baseball bat—and miss! Or shoot a goal during a hockey game—and miss! And what about running with the football for a touchdown—and fumbling it?**

• **What sports do you like to play? What mistakes worry you and keep you from playing your best?**
• **How would a kind word from a teammate help a no-good-pretty-bad-game day?**

Professional sportsmen and women have bad game days. For them to perform well the next time around, they listen to their coaches. The coach tells them to shake it off and try again. Worry buster #2: A kind word from a coach or mentor goes a long way to help lift doubt and worry. Repeat Proverbs 12:25 again with your children.

Finally, ask a volunteer to pull item three, the watch, from your pocket. **Having too little time is a big worry for children. With busy schedules, the worry is that there won't be enough time in the day to get everything done.**

• **Being anxious won't put more minutes in your day. What can someone say to you that would help ease a time crunch worry?**

Worry buster #3: I agree! A smile and encouraging word from a friend or brother or sister can help you relax. Go ahead and get done what you can do. Leave the rest for another day. Repeat Proverbs 12:25 one last time before your children exit. **Remember, a kind word is a "worry buster" and will lift the spirits of those you care about.**

If you wish, add additional items to your apron and extend your sermon on kid worries. A key can represent being home alone or loneliness; a handheld calculator, the worry over bad grades. A thermometer can begin a talk on sickness or feeling blue.

Blowin' in the Wind

On Your Mark

Bible Truth: God wants us to encourage each other.

Bible Verse: A cheerful heart is good medicine, **but** a crushed spirit dries up the bones (Prov. 17:22).

Godprint: Empathy

Get Set

You'll need chalk, a rock or something else to crush it, and a container to put it in. Mark Proverbs 17:22 in a Bible.

GO!

Hold up a piece of chalk. What do I have in my hand? *(Chalk.)* **What do we use chalk for?** *(Writing on a chalkboard.)* **Have you ever had the job of cleaning the chalkboard or the erasers? What do you find when you do that job?** *(Chalk dust.)* **When we write on a chalkboard, we don't even think about how we're leaving behind dust. Let's think about that for a minute while we do something else with this piece of chalk.**

Invite one or more of the kids to help grind up the chalk to a find powder. Make sure it is thoroughly crushed.

• **Now what do we have here?** *(Chalk dust.)*
• **Is this any good for anything? Can we use it to write on the board?**

Put a small amount of chalk dust in your hand. Ask one or two of the younger kids to blow the chalk dust out of your hand.

• **Now where is the chalk?** *(It's blown all around. It's not really chalk anymore.)*

We crushed the chalk and it dried up and blew away. It's never going to be a stick of chalk again, is it? It's pretty easy to crush chalk and blow it away. Let's read a Bible verse about something else that is easy to crush. Ask a volunteer to read Proverbs 17:22.

A cheerful heart is good medicine, but a crushed spirit dries up the bones.

- What does this verse say a cheerful heart is like? *(Good medicine.)*
- Why is medicine good for you? *(It makes you well.)*
- What is a crushed spirit like? *(Dried-up bones.)*
- How do you think a spirit could get crushed? *(When someone says something mean to you. When you feel really sad about something.)*

I see one small little word that makes a big difference in this verse. Can you guess what it is? *(But.)* When we have cheerful hearts, we feel better about things. It's like we've taken the right medicine to get well. And our cheerful hearts also make other people feel better.

Here comes the little word: but. If we're not careful, our cranky and crabby hearts can crush someone else's spirit so it's like dried-up bones. God wants us to encourage each other, not crush each other's spirits the way we crushed this chalk. So let's take our good medicine and keep our hearts cheerful.

Bow for prayer. **Lord, our hearts are cheerful because we know you and you love us. When we start to feel discouraged or sad, cheer us up with your love. Then please help us to spread that cheer to others. In Jesus' name, amen.**

Of Calendars and Lists

On Your Mark

Bible Truth: God wants us to follow his plans.
Bible Verse: Many are the plans in a man's heart, **but** it is the LORD's purpose that prevails (Prov. 19:21).
Godprint: Purposefulness

Get Set

You'll need a marker and an assortment of small tools, cleaning supplies, bags, and instruction books. At the top of a large sheet of paper, write "To Do." Mark Proverbs 19:21 in a Bible.

GO!

As kids gather, load yourself up with your supplies, making it hard for you to juggle everything. Keep a grip on your To Do list. With exasperation, let everything tumble from your arms to the floor in front of the children.

I just don't see how I'm going to get this all done. I've got to clean the house, and fix the back door, and pack for our family vacation, and the toaster isn't working right—how am I ever going to get it all done? Do you think any of you could help me? Start passing out the various items in your collection. **Here, you look like you're handy with tools. And you, I just know you're a scrubber dubber super duper cleaner. And I know you like to read, so you can figure out all these instructions. Fit Tab A into Slot B—I never can figure out that stuff.** Continue until you have passed out everything except the To Do list.

Okay, everyone, let's get busy. What, you don't know what you should do now?

Sometimes we get too busy with all the things we have to do or all the things we'd like to do. Let's make a "To Do" list of things that make our lives busy. Tell me some things that all the people in your family are busy with. Invite kids to suggest items and write them on your list. Encourage as many children to participate as possible. They may mention examples of: schoolwork, sports practices, music lessons, parents' jobs, household chores, yard work, travel, shopping.

I would guess that most of you have a calendar in your house where your parents write down the things that your family does. You might like to ask adults in the congregation to hold up personal planners that they carry with them.

- **Can you think of a time when you planned to do something, and then you had to change your plans?**
- **How did you feel about changing your plans?**

The Bible has a verse that helps us understand something important about the plans that we make. Ask a volunteer to read Proverbs 19:21.

> **Many are the plans in a man's heart, but it is the LORD's purpose that prevails.**

- **What does this verse say about the plans we have in our hearts?** *(They are many.)*
- **Can anyone tell us what "prevail" means?** *(To be the strongest.)*
- **Why is it important to know what the Lord's plans are for us?**

We make decisions every day about how to spend our time and money. This verse reminds us that no matter how many plans we have, the only one that matters is God's plan for us.

Bow for prayer. **God, thank you for making plans for our lives. Thank you that you have a purpose for each of us. When we get too busy or think the wrong things are important, remind us that your plan is the only one that matters. In Jesus' name, amen.**

Love on the HorizSon

On Your Mark

Bible Truth: God's power and magnificence will last forever.
Bible Verse: Heaven and earth will pass away, **but** my words will never pass away (Luke 21:33).
Godprint: Wonder

Get Set

Bible, long strip of paper about two inches wide, tape, highlighter, beach ball, star stickers. Mark Luke 21:33 in a Bible.

GO!

• Define the word *forever* using your own words.
• Have you ever said, "This is taking forever!" ? What are some things in your everyday life that seem to take forever?
• Can you think of something that would help a little child understand the idea of *forever*?

As you talk, take the length of paper and twist it once. Tape the ends together. **Waiting for a birthday party or a vacation trip can seem to take forever. We use the word forever to mean a long, long time.**

This twisted strip of paper is known as a Möbius strip. Named for the man who created it, August Ferdinand Möbius, a 19th-century German mathematician and astronomer, this paper twist has one continuous side. Pick up the highlighter and draw a line starting at the center of the strip. Continue drawing until the line connects with its beginning. **It appears as if the strip has no end. I could go on drawing this line for a long, long time. But eventually I would grow tired and stop. Not God. When God uses the word *forever* he means eternity, a time without end.**

• **What does God give us that will last for eternity?** *(His holy Word.)*

Ask children to join their thumb and pointer finger to form a circle. Using the pointer finger on their other hand, have them trace inside the circle.

A circle has no beginning or end. It goes around and around and around. It's a good way for us to think about forever.

Hold up the beach ball. **We can think of this beach ball as the earth.** Try and spin the ball on your finger. **God's Word tell us that someday the earth, like the leaves on an autumn tree, will pass away. God will take care of us when that happens so we don't need to worry. But he tells us the earth is not a forever thing.** Hand a volunteer the star stickers and ask them to stick two or three stickers to the ball. Throw the ball up into the air. **The heavens, the sky, and the stars above it will pass away too. We know this to be true because God's Word says so. The heavens are not a forever thing.**

Open your Bible and read Luke 21:33. Then ask your group to repeat Luke 21:33 with you.

> **Heaven and earth will pass away, but my words will never pass away.**

So what will outlast the earth and the sky and the millions of twinkly stars? God's Word. His Word tell us that his power and splendor, brilliance and majesty last forever. It's a wonderful and amazing thing to know that the Word of God is perfectly right for the past, the present, and the future.

Throw the beach ball out into the group and have them try and keep it up and in motion without it falling to the floor.

Shine, Jesus, Shine

On Your Mark

Bible Truth: God wants us to shine the light of Jesus into a dark world.
Bible Verse: The light shines in the darkness, **but** the darkness has not understood it (John 1:5).
Godprint: Evangelism

Get Set

You'll need several small mirrors and a flashlight. Mark John 1:5 in a Bible.

GO!

How well can you see? Some of us wear glasses to help us see better, but I think we'd all agree that it's easier to see in the light than in the darkness. **Have you ever bumped into something in the dark because you could not see it?** Pause to let kids respond. **Let's do a little experiment to see how light helps us see.**

Hand small mirrors to several of them. Arrange the mirrors so they're all angled off each other and will reflect light to each other. Then shine the flashlight directly into one mirror only.

- **I'm shining the flashlight into one mirror. What do you see in the other mirrors?**
  (The light reflects.)
- **Do you think darkness is stronger than light or light is stronger than darkness?**

If we did our experiment with mirrors and a flashlight in a dark room, with one flashlight we could make enough light to send the darkness running. The light would overcome the darkness.

Now I'm going to say something really important about light, so I want you to listen carefully. Okay? This is a message you don't want to miss. Say the Bible verse in pig latin.

E-thay ight-lay ines-shay in-way e-thay arkness-day, ut-bay e-thay arkness-day as-hay ot-nay understood-way it-way.

Wow, I'm glad I got to say that. Now we all know, right? Maybe you should say it back to me

just to make sure you really got it. Pause to see if kids will try. Some of the older kids may recognize that you were speaking pig latin. **Can anyone explain that important message for us? No? I'll give you a clue. We can find the answer in the Bible.** Ask a volunteer to read John 1:5.

The light shines in the darkness, but the darkness has not understood it.

Ah, there it is in plain English!

• What do you think it means for darkness to understand light?

That's a hard one, isn't it? At Christmastime we decorate with stars. Do you ever wonder why that is? This verse is one of the reasons. Jesus came into a dark, sinful world with the light of God. The world didn't understand why Jesus came. God gave us his Word, the Bible, so we could understand why Jesus came. We don't have to spend the rest of our lives in darkness. We can live in the light of Jesus and reflect it to the people all around us.

Bow for prayer. **Lord Jesus, we're so glad that you came to earth as a baby. You came into the world as a shining light that no darkness can put out. Shine through us so that other people can see your light in us. Amen.**

It's in the Bag

On Your Mark

Bible Truth: God wants us to share what we have with others.
Bible Verse: All the believers were one in heart and mind. No one claimed that any of his possessions was his own, **but** they shared everything they had (Acts 4:32).
Godprint: Cooperation

Get Set

You'll need a cloth bag or pillowcase filled with "cool" items that children want to own. For example, a handheld electronic game and/or controller to a video game system, plush animal, soccer ball, cellular phone, new board game, books, DVDs, a popular snack, a special mug, wallet, etc. Mark Acts 4:32 in a Bible.

GO!

We have houses filled to the brim with lots of things—some are old, some gently used, and a few items are our "new stuff," which we wouldn't want to part with for all the world!

• **What is your most cherished belonging? How long have you had it? What makes it so?**
• **What was your most cherished thing *last* year?**

In my bag are items that most kids would love to have. Ask for a volunteer. **I'd like you, Sammy** (substitute the name of your child), **to feel the bag from the outside and grab hold of one item. See if your fingertips can guess what it is!** Hold the item-filled bag in front of you. Ask your volunteer to identify the item before you pull it out to show the group.

Great job! I think we can say that if your computer game is the newest thing out there, your brother or sister or friend would want to play with it too.

Today's Scripture verse comes from the Book of Acts. Hand your Bible to a volunteer and ask him or her to read Acts 4:32.

All the believers were one in heart and mind. No one claimed that any of his possessions was his own, but they shared everything they had.

Hmm. Imagine opening your home to all the neighborhood children and having them play with anything they wanted. Maybe even fix themselves a snack of your favorite cereal, cookies, or chips!

• How would you feel about sharing the very best things you own with neighbors on your street?
• Would you declare "off-limits" to the best and newest games and toys?

Again, hold the bag filled with items in front of you. Ask a volunteer in your group to come up and feel the bag. Ask if they can identify the item before you pull it out.

In Acts 4:32, believers were willing to help and share with one another because of their love and commitment to Christ. Without this harmony or spiritual unity, the early church could not have survived. Bickering and selfishness do not hold people together—coming together in Christ does.

• Can you think of a time when selfishness ended a friendship or caused an argument with a brother, sister, or cousin?
• How can we crush the selfish feeling inside when a friend wants a turn on our new bike? (With Christ's help, we can put on his loving nature and share what we have with others.)

Ask for three or four volunteers, depending on the items left in your bag, and see if they can identify what they feel.

Today's Scripture is not asking the impossible. God's Word tells us that who we are and what we own belong to God. Think of your body and your skills as things on loan from him—much like the books you check out from the library. You don't own the book. You're simply borrowing it for a little while. When we cooperate and share our things, we share what God has already given us: his abundant blessings.

Show Me the Money

On Your Mark

Bible Truth: God gives us the free gift of eternal life.
Bible Verse: For the wages of sin is death, **but** the gift of God is eternal life in Christ Jesus our Lord (Rom. 6:23).
Godprint: Repentance

Get Set

You'll need some play paper money from a hobby store or a board game. Mark Romans 6:23 in a Bible.

GO!

As kids gather, shuffle the paper money in you hands, giving the impression that you have a great deal. **Wow, I've got so much money here. I feel like I could buy anything I want with all this money. It's my money, and I can do anything with it that I want to do. I think I'll give you a chance to earn some of this money. Anyone who wants 20 dollars, stand up and do 10 jumping jacks.** Pass out bills to kids who do this. **Now if you want 50 dollars, let me see 10 sit-ups.** Pass out bills to kids who attempt this. **Now how about a 100? Let's see 10 push-ups.** Pause to pass out bills.

You all worked hard and earned the money I've given you. Congratulations! Now I'm feeling generous—but just for a few of you. Choose a couple of kids and give them all the money you have left. Kids who did not even attempt any of the exercises are a perfect choice at this point!

Everyone got what's fair, right? No doubt you'll encounter objections to that statement. **Oh, you don't think _____ and _____** (name the children you gave the last of your money to) **earned all that extra money? Well, maybe not. Sometimes we receive something that's just a gift, even if we don't deserve it. Let's read a Bible verse about that.**

Ask a volunteer to read Romans 6:23.

> For the wages of sin is death, but the gift of God is eternal life in Christ Jesus our Lord.

• **Who can tell me what "wages" means?** *(Pay; what you earn.)*

- What does this verse say that we earn by our sin? *(Death.)*
- What's the difference between wages and a gift? *(You earn your wages by your work. You don't do anything to deserve or earn a gift.)*
- What little tiny word in this verse is very important to pay attention to? *(But. It means just the opposite is about to happen. We deserve death, but God gives us life.)*

When we sin, we get just what we deserve. But God offers us a free gift. When we decide to let God change us from the inside out, he helps us live our lives the way he wants us to live, not in our selfish, sinful ways. When we repent, we turn around and live God's way, with the promise that we can live with God forever. We have eternal life! We don't do anything to earn eternal life. But God gives it to us as a free gift. Let's thank him for that.

Bow for prayer. **God, thank you for not giving us what we deserve. Thank you for giving us a gift instead, the gift of eternal life. We want to show our thankfulness for this gift by living your way. Thank you for helping us to do that. In Jesus' name, amen.**

If you don't need your paper money back, let kids know that they can keep it as a reminder of God's free gift of eternal life—something they can't buy, no matter how much money they have.

Overcomers Unanimous

On Your Mark

Bible Truth: God wants us to respond to others with his goodness.
Bible Verse: Do not be overcome by evil, **but** overcome evil with good (Rom. 12:21).
Godprint: Faithfulness

Get Set

You'll need a checkerboard and game pieces and a watch with a second hand. Mark Romans 12:21 in a Bible.

GO!

As kids gather, open up the checkerboard and begin putting the pieces in place. **How many of you like to play checkers? Who do you like to play checkers with?** Pause for responses.

We're going to need a couple of volunteers for a game of checkers right now. Choose two players and have them move near the board.

This game of checkers will have one special rule. You have to think fast, because we're only going to play for 30 seconds. (If you have more time, play for one minute, or offer another pair an opportunity to play.)

After the game, talk about:

• **What's the goal of checkers?** (*To capture the other player's pieces. To get your pieces to the other side and get crowned.*)
• **How does it feel when you jump a player's piece and capture it?**
• **How does it feel when you get jumped?**

What if we said that the red checkers were good and the black checkers were evil? When a black piece jumps a red piece, which side is winning? (*Evil.*) **How about when a red jumps a black?** (*Good is winning.*) **That reminds me of a Bible verse. Let's read it.** Ask a volunteer to read Romans 12:21.

Do not be overcome by evil, but overcome evil with good.

• What does "overcome" mean? *(To win; to capture.)*
• Which checker does God want us to be like? *(Red.)*
• According to this verse, how should we respond when someone does something that hurts us?
• Tell me one thing that is hard about overcoming evil with good.

Remember our special rule for the checkers game—thinking fast? When something bad happens to us, we usually react right away. God wants us to think fast, but think good. Right now I want you to think fast about ways that you can overcome evil with good. When I say "Go," you call out ways to show goodness even when bad things happen. Ready? Go! Let kids call out ideas all at once for a few seconds. Acknowledge all the great ideas.

God is faithful to us, even when bad things happen. When we overcome evil with good, we're faithful to God. I hope that the next time you play checkers and you are jumping the other person's pieces, you'll think about this Bible verse and remember to overcome evil with good.

Bow for prayer. **Lord, thank you that you are always good. We want to be faithful to you and respond with goodness when bad things happen to us. Thank you for helping us do this. In Jesus' name, amen.**

Illuminating Kindness

On Your Mark

Bible Truth: God wants us to be kind to everyone.

Bible Verse: Make sure that nobody pays back wrong for wrong, **but** always try to be kind to each other and to everyone else (1 Thess. 5:15).

Godprint: Kindness

Get Set

You'll need six-inch cardboard circles or heavy-duty paper plates, heavy-duty aluminum foil, and glue. Mark 1 Thessalonians 5:15 in a Bible.

GO!

Before the day of your sermon, make simple mirrors. Cut out small cardboard circles (or cut away the ribbed portion of paper plates, leaving just the center circles). Cut the same size circles from heavy-duty aluminum foil. Glue the dull side of the foil to the cardboard circles carefully so as not to crease the foil. Have enough mirror circles on hand for everyone in your group, plus a few for visitors.

• How tempting is it to want to hurt others when they hurt us or someone we care about?
• Do you think **kindness** can be the answer to someone who hurts you? Why or why not?

The Apostle Paul wanted all the Christians of Thessalonica to hear his letter of encouragement. In it, he writes keep up the faith, live to please God, love others, and avoid temptation. As we know, however, wanting to hurt others when we are wronged is a pretty big temptation.

Open your Bible to 1 Thessalonians 5:15 and read the Scripture aloud.

> Make sure that nobody pays back wrong for wrong, but always try to be kind to each other and to everyone else.

Kindness doesn't seem the right answer, does it, when harsh words or angry fists would take care of things for us? In a sinful world it's hard to be a Christian citizen. But as a community of believers we want others to come to Jesus and be filled with his love.

Striking back or hurting others will not bring people to Jesus Christ.

• Share a time when you felt helpless to assist someone you loved. Did you think to lift it up in prayer? What about next time?
• What do you think the Apostle Paul's reaction was every time he was whipped, beaten, and thrown into prison for preaching about Christ? Why didn't he fight back or seek revenge?

God knew all about the struggles of the young church of Thessalonica. God sent the words of Paul to help encourage them. When we are hurt by others and need encouragement, God sends moms and dads, friends and neighbors, teachers and pastors to come to our rescue. In their wisdom, they can help us sort out the trouble without taking revenge.

• Are there special words you always use in prayer to tell God that you need his help? Or do you prefer to talk as you go?

Distribute the foil circles you prepared before class. Have children take a look at their blurry smiles! **I'd like you to engrave the shiny side of the foil using your fingernail. Start by outlining the simple mirror with a decorative border of small circles or swirls.** Pause as children work. **In the center mark a bold cross. Let the cross always remind you that Jesus' death on the cross paid the price for all sin, including our desire to "get even" with others. Instead, let's reflect God's forgiven love.**

Megahurtz

On Your Mark

Bible Truth: Bad things happen to everyone, even those who follow Jesus, but God is with us.

Bible Verse: A righteous man may have many troubles, **but** the LORD delivers him from them all (Ps. 34:19).

Godprint: Commitment

Get Set

You'll need copies of the Comfort Me Quilt reproducible on page 106 and pencils. Optional: brightly colored paper strips, scissors, glue sticks. Mark Psalm 34:19 in a Bible.

GO!

· What troubles, disappointments, or frustrations did you face this week?
· How do these times make you feel?

Today's truth tells us that bad things happen to everyone, even those who follow Jesus. But we needn't spend time worrying over our troubles or even how to escape from them. Why? Because God is with us. He'll decide when we will be delivered from trouble and just how long we must endure the tough time.

· Why do you think God allows troubles to happen to good and honest people, those who have faith in him? *(To test or challenge; to increase faithfulness, perseverance, and wisdom; to accept his will.)*

Whatever God's decision, he commits to us and makes a promise that no matter what happens he has us "covered" in love. He will protect, secure, and deliver his faithful from loss, heartache, and failure. This is a promise that only a powerful and wise God can make—and keep.

Open your Bible to Psalm 34:19 and read it aloud.

A righteous man may have many troubles, but the LORD delivers him from them all.

Distribute the Comfort Me Quilt handouts. **Let's reinforce today's Scripture verse with today's handout.**

• **Lots of people worry about things when they settle in bed at night. Often it keeps them from falling asleep. Has this ever happened to you?**
• **Does a comfy blanket or quilt make you feel warm and protected on chilly nights? How can this remind you of God's comfort in times of trouble?**

When you go home, pick up a pencil and fill in the blank patches on your quilt handout with worries or troubles that make you feel unsettled. Then finish your Comfort Me Quilt with the names of people and things that make you feel safe and secure. Ask your mom or dad to pray with you.

Even when storms crash, parents bicker, or the dog chews your spelling homework, you belong to God and can feel secure in his care.

If you are in a setting where children can work on the Comfort Me Quilt while you're together, distribute scissors and have children make linear cuts in their quilt handouts where indicated by the bold, solid cutting lines. Be sure to stop at the dots. Weave colorful paper strips in and out of the cut handout to personalize the quilts. Glue down ends to keep the quilt secure.

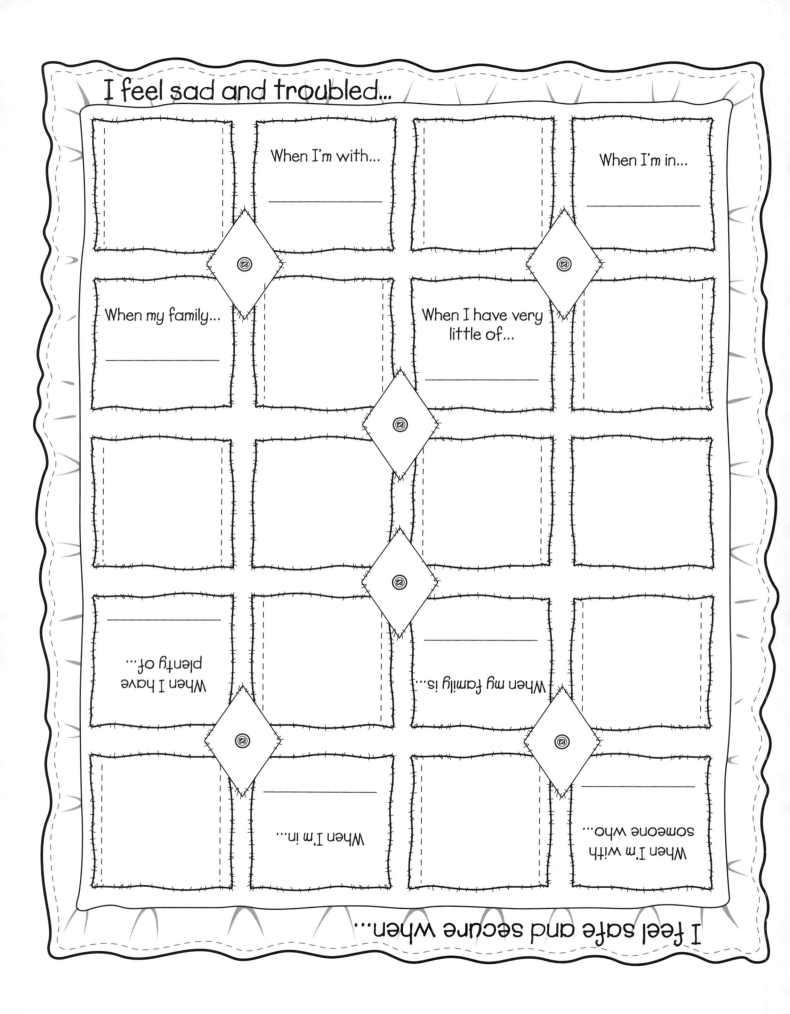

I feel sad and troubled...

When I'm with...
_____

When I'm in...
_____

When my family...
_____

When I have very little of...
_____

When I have plenty of...
_____

When my family is...
_____

When I'm in...
_____

When I'm with someone who...
_____

I feel safe and secure when...

Godprints Kids Can Learn

Commitment: Choose to follow Jesus and live a life that honors God.

Community: Be part of a group of people who come together because they love God and want to worship and serve him.

Compassion: Be aware of another person's needs, particularly during times of unhappiness. Share God's love with someone who needs it.

Cooperation: Work with others to do what God wants you to do together, instead of just doing what you want.

Confidence: Because you trust in God, you can be sure of your ability to do what he wants you to do, even when it's hard.

Conviction: Don't let anything shake your faith in God. Act in ways that show your faith is not easily shaken.

Courage: Stand firm when you face danger or pressure, because God gives you strength.

Discipleship: Learn from Jesus, and show what you've learned in your attitudes and actions.

Empathy: Jesus knows exactly how we feel and he helps us know how someone else feels.

Evangelism: Tell the good news of Jesus to other people because God wants everyone to know him.

Faith: Believe what God has said about himself. Respond to the relationship he offers. Then make choices that show that you know God personally.

Faithfulness: God is always faithful to us. Make choices that please God and show that you want to do his will.

Forgiveness: We forgive others because God forgives us. You can pardon someone who has hurt you.

Friendliness: Show that you want to have a relationship with another person, just the way God wants to have a relationship with you. Do what's good for the other person.

Honesty: God is always truthful. We should be truthful too, and not try to hide the truth by lying or leaving some things out.

Hope: God is in control of your life and your future. He makes good things happen even from bad things.

Integrity: Show that God has made you a new creation in Christ Jesus by making choices that show that you're new from the inside out.

Kindness: An attitude that shows a true spirit of helpfulness toward other people, just as God is helpful to us.

Obedience: Follow what God tells you to do in the Bible and by his Holy Spirit.

Praise: Honor God's greatness by what you say and do.

Prayerfulness: Remember that the presence and power of God is with you in every situation. When you call on God, he answers.

Preciousness: God made you in his image! Can you feel how much you matter to God and how much he loves you?

Purposefulness: God has a purpose and a plan for you, no matter how old you are.

Repentance: You can choose to turn away from sin and selfishness and be more like Jesus.

Reverence: Respond to God in a way that shows you respect him for his greatness and power.

Thankfulness: Remember to appreciate that God loves you and everything he does for you.

Trust: You can depend on God completely because he never lets you down.

Wisdom: Use the skills, knowledge, and judgment that God gives you in ways that honor him.

Wonder: God is amazing! Admire his power and magnificence.

Worship: God is worthy of our highest honor, attention, and praise. Show that you believe this by what you say and do.

Index of Scripture References

Index of Topics

The Word at Work . . . Around the World

What would you do if you wanted to share God's love with children on the streets of your city? That's the dilemma David C. Cook faced in 1870s Chicago. His answer was to create literature that would capture children's hearts.

Out of those humble beginnings grew a worldwide ministry that has used literature to proclaim God's love and disciple generation after generation. Cook Communications Ministries is committed to personal discipleship—to helping people of all ages learn God's Word, embrace his salvation, walk in his ways, and minister in his name.

Opportunities—and Crisis

We live in a land of plenty—including plenty of Christian literature! But what about the rest of the world? Jesus commanded, "Go and make disciples of all nations" (Matt. 28:19) and we want to obey this commandment. But how does a publishing organization "go" into all the world?

There are five times as many Christians around the world as there are in North America. Christian workers in many of these countries have no more than a New Testament, or perhaps a single shared copy of the Bible, from which to learn and teach.

We are committed to sharing what God has given us with such Christians.

A vital part of Cook Communications Ministries is our international outreach, Cook Communications Ministries International (CCMI). Your purchase of this book, and of other books and Christian-growth products from Cook, enables CCMI to provide Bibles and Christian literature to people in more than 150 languages in 65 countries.

Cook Communications Ministries is a not-for-profit, self-supporting organization. Revenues from sales of our books, Bible curriculum, and other church and home products not only fund our U.S. ministry, but also fund our CCMI ministry around the world. One hundred percent of donations to CCMI go to our international literature programs.

CCMI reaches out internationally in three ways:

· Our premier International Christian Publishing Institute (ICPI) trains leaders from nationally led publishing houses around the world to develop evangelism and discipleship materials to transform lives in their countries.

· We provide literature for pastors, evangelists, and Christian workers in their national language. We provide study helps for pastors and lay leaders in many parts of the world, such as China, India, Cuba, Iran, and Vietnam.

· We reach people at risk—refugees, AIDS victims, street children, and famine victims—with God's Word. CCMI puts literature that shares the Good News into the hands of people at spiritual risk—people who might die before they hear the name of Jesus and are transformed by his love.

Word Power—God's Power

Faith Kidz, RiverOak, Honor, Life Journey, Victor, NexGen — every time you purchase a book produced by Cook Communications Ministries, you not only meet a vital personal need in your life or in the life of someone you love, but you're also a part of ministering to José in Colombia, Humberto in Chile, Gousa in India, or Lidiane in Brazil. You help make it possible for a pastor in China, a child in Peru, or a mother in West Africa to enjoy a life-changing book. And because you helped, children and adults around the world are learning God's Word and walking in his ways.

Thank you for your partnership in helping to disciple the world. May God bless you with the power of his Word in your life.

For more information about our international ministries, visit www.ccmi.org.

A New Title in the Bible FUNstuff series:
Bible Crafts For All Seasons

0-78144-205-2 • Item # 104024

Bible Crafts For All Seasons

Bible Crafts for All Seasons provides teachers with more than 50 unique crafts that are flexible enough to be used with a large or small group and that only require simple, inexpensive supplies. Teachers select the difficulty level to fit the skill-level of the class! Covering not only major holidays and seasons, but also special days such as birthdays, Grandparents Day, and more.

Find These and Other Great Cook Products at Your Local Christian Bookstore